Are You TOO STRESSED To Be BLESSED?

21 PRACTICAL WAYS YOU CAN POSITION YOURSELF TO BE BLESSED BY GOD

Doug Kelley

ISBN: 1519378351
ISBN-13: 978-1519378354

Dedication

As this first book comes forth, I feel compelled to honor "my person." She is known throughout the world as my best friend who carries me forward with her love and never-ending willingness to do anything that needs to be done.

With my wife I used to watch a chick flick on television about doctors (Grey's Anatomy). One of the woman doctors would always refer to another of the woman doctors as "my person." It was cute, possessive and meaningful.

It made me think that we all need "a person." We need somebody that we can share our darkest secrets, our deepest fears and our lonely moments. We need somebody who really "gets us" and still sticks around.

I won the lottery when I married my wife, as she is truly "my person." I don't own her or control her. I can't even extract a correct opinion out of her. As she ages she has become more independent. But, no matter what our disagreements might be over the little, everyday things, she is "my person."

The Bible says there is "a friend that sticks closer than a brother" (Prov 18:24). Of course, we can interpret this as Jesus. But, it is comforting to have a "person" who listens and loves no matter what. My person is always willing to listen and love. I pray that I can be that person for her and others.

So, with great joy I dedicate this first of many books to the hardest working, most loving person that I have ever known – Cathy Dean Kelley.

Acknowledgement

I would like to give a special shout out to my great friend John Syratt who spent hundreds of hours editing *Are You Too Stressed to Be Blessed?* He is far more gifted in linguistic consistency than I am. I have a tendency to just "get it done." One of John's gifts is to get it right. Thank you John for your effort to make a good book great.

I also want to thank my brother Don Kelley and friend for life Jeff Monfort who spent hours pouring through a rough manuscript and suggesting needed changes. I am forever grateful.

And last but not least is my wife Cathy. The people at Open Arms call her "The First Lady." Although she dislikes the term, she is the first lady in everything important. She has formatted, re-formatted, slaved over drop quotes and learned the requirements of publishing a book. May God give us many more years and many more books.

...DougKelley

...November30,2015

Contents

Introduction

IT WAS MY HIGH SCHOOL GRADUATION and I was excited to close this chapter of my life and move on to the next chapter. I was waiting for my name to be called.

The Superintendent of North Toole County High School in Sunburst, Montana always shared a few kind words about the graduate before handing out the diploma. With only 32 graduates, each senior was given a few carefully chosen words to facilitate their transfer from high school to whatever was next in their life.

High school had been a blur of activity and various accomplishments. I had lettered nine times in three different sports, been co-editor of the school paper, president of the Lettermen's Club, and winner of the local oratory contest.

On the negative side, I managed to scrape by with barely passable grades in Latin, Algebra and Geometry. I ranked a solid fifteen out of thirty-two in my class, as girls, sports and friends were far more important than good grades.

"...Doug has been the most controversial student who has ever come through the doors...."

Now was my moment to leave the nest and get on with my dream to become the next Perry Mason – the master of the courtroom. Perry Mason might have been just a television rendition of the perfect lawyer but I could reach for the stars and become that lawyer. My Dad had taught me to dream big. He preached to his family the "can do anything" gospel of work and sacrifice.

A modest scholarship induced me to commit to a small Catholic college two hours from home. I could hardly wait to make new friends and meet new challenges.

As my name, Douglas B. Kelley, was announced, I eagerly moved forward to receive my diploma. As I approached the podium, the Superintendent appeared to be at a loss for words.

Finally, he said, "I don't really know what to say about this next student except that Doug has been the MOST CONTROVERSIAL STUDENT who has ever come through the doors of our high school."

I was not sure if the Superintendent had pronounced a blessing or a curse. I took my diploma, waved at my family and joined the rest of my class.

The Superintendent was not oblivious to my tenure as the head of the Lettermen's Club that went overboard in initiating new members or the editorials I had written critical of the school administration or my effort to change the name of the school mascot.

It was a small step that would ultimately lead me to seven years of college, marriage to Cathy Dean and multiple occupations – lawyer, pastor, personnel business owner, travel agency owner, restaurant, marina owner and real estate investor.

Little did I know that my life would be full of zigs and zags – from altar boy to born again, from doubting Doug to Pastor Doug, from prosecuting attorney to pastor of broken-hearted drug addicts, alcoholics, prostitutes and criminals, from fifty years in majestic Montana to the chaos and confusion of California.

Through all the changes and challenges, controversies have followed me like a barking dog. This is a story about more than a barking dog named controversy. It's a story about God's blessing in spite of controversy

Over the years I have thought about the label "most controversial student" as my life has been filled with conflicts, controversy and challenges. Was it a curse? Was it a harmless assessment intended to reprimand me? Or was it a secular prophecy that would be fulfilled countless times in my life?

Lawyers are quick to ask a judge to take judicial notice of indisputable facts. There are three things concerning blessing of which we should take judicial notice. These apply to everybody regardless of ethnicity, economics, religion or gender.

First, everybody wants to be blessed. We wake up hoping and praying that today will be our lucky day. We will meet the person of our dreams, get the promotion that we desperately want, win the lottery or be more loved and appreciated than anybody, anywhere.

Second, everybody is not blessed. Not everybody gets the blessing, the girl, the job, the lottery or whatever else that represents blessing. Many of us grab for the gold and catch a handful of dust. We are the people with the thorn poking us in our side.

Third, God wants to bless us. The Bible says that the eye of the Lord goes looking for somebody to bless. Many of us are like the little kid waving our arm vigorously in the air while we holler as loud as we can, "Choose me, choose me!"

When the Lord gave a blessing to Jacob, his brother Esau cried for all the unblessed of the world, "Is there not a blessing for me too?"

It's not God's will that any man die unloved and unsaved. God wants all men to know Him, as He created man in His image and likeness. We are just like God – sovereign.

We use the words "free will" to express our understanding of our ability to choose a blessing or a curse. God puts before us blessing or cursing, life or death, and then stands by and says, "Choose."

"Is there not a blessing for me too?"

I recently finished a year that was more of a curse than a blessing. I like to prophetically label years and then try to fulfill the lofty label. Honesty demands looking back and judging each year on the basis of what actually happened.

Many years ago when I had completed a very bad year (church split, brother leaving me, etc.), I joyfully announced to the church, "Happy Days are Here Again." Wrong! Wrong! Wrong! Instead of happy days, we had more painful days that needed to be endured.

As 2010 was coming to a close, I was visiting with Kert Evans, my church administrator. Knowing how he liked to historically label the years – the year of the building, the year of Arms of Praise, etc. I told him that I had a label for 2010.

We all experience Heaven and Hell every year (sometimes every day).

"What do you think 2010 was?" asked Kert.

"It was a HELL of a year. With four lawsuits, a broken relationship, and all the money spent on lawyers and buildings, I am lucky to be alive," I exclaimed. "Building inspectors, bills and bureaucrats have made my life a living Hell on earth."

"I don't agree. I think 2010 was the year of the House of Hope. Look what we were able to get done this past year," pointed out Kert.

"I can't believe that the man my wife calls the 'most negative man who ever lived' is more positive than me. You are right. We had some great accomplishments that were birthed in the midst of tribulation," I conceded.

Who was right? Who was wrong? Was it possible that we were both right? It had been a year filled with both Hell and Heaven. The truth is that we all experience Heaven and Hell every year (sometimes every day).

The Bible tells a story about two men – a poor man named Lazarus and an unnamed rich man. The poor man lived at the gate of the rich man and ate scraps from the rich man's table as dogs licked his wounds.

The rich man was blessed while Lazarus was unblessed. One experienced Heaven on earth and the other Hell on earth, and then they died.

The poor man went to Heaven and sat on the lap of Abraham, while the rich man went to Hell. The Bible records a remarkable dialogue.

"Send me Lazarus with a cold drink," cried the rich man. "It is hotter than Hell (my interpretation) and I am suffering greatly."

"It's impossible, as there is a big gulf between Heaven and Hell," responded Abraham.

"Well, send somebody to warn my brothers as they don't want to come here," asked the tormented rich man.

Hell is a place of torment, suffering and separation. The rich man was tormented as a result of his short-sighted decisions that led him to a place of eternal suffering and separation.

Hell is not a nice place. In his arrogance, the atheist claims that there is no God. The Bible says, "The fool says in his heart there is no God."

The rain falls on the just and the unjust. Many come to Christ with the hope that they will never suffer. Jesus said, "All that will live godly will suffer persecution."

When suffering (or Hell) comes, the new believer can become confused and derailed. He is quick to ask, "Where is God?" Job is an exception to this generalization. When

Job began to suffer, his wife argued that Job should "curse God and die."

But Job remained steadfast in his belief in the goodness and righteousness of God. Job said, "The Lord gives and the Lord takes away. Blessed be the name of the Lord." Job had a Heaven perspective when he said, "Naked we came into this world and naked we will leave."

So, blessing is Heaven on earth while suffering is Hell on earth. When I have money, it is Heaven on earth. When I am broke and can't pay my bills, it is Hell on earth. Jesus taught His disciples to pray for Heaven on earth - "Thy will be done on earth as it is in Heaven." There are no broken relationships, sickness or bills in Heaven.

This book is intended to help you position yourself for blessing.

The Bible says that there is more to be learned from the house of sorrow than the house of joy and gladness. I have never gone willingly to the house of sorrow but have been dragged there kicking and screaming.

This book is intended to help you position yourself for blessing. If you want to take a shower and wash away the dirt and sweat of the day, you need to get under the showerhead. You don't stand in the toilet bowl and complain that you are not blessed. You get yourself under the showerhead and turn on the water believing that you will be blessed with a clean body.

Some Christians over-spiritualize the entire concept of blessing. They put 100% of the responsibility on God. They are standing in the toilet bowl wanting a shower. God has specific things to say that will bring blessing. We must POSITION OURSELVES FOR BLESSING.

1

A Dark Night in the Ghetto

Position for Blessing - Take Action

DO YOU REMEMBER ME? said the man as he pressed physically into my space. He looked familiar but I could not place him. I admitted that I was unsure though he looked familiar.

"I'm the guy who came to your church with a gun. Now, do you remember me?"

"Yeah, I remember. That was a few years ago." I remember somebody running up to me in a panic, crying, "Phil brought a gun and is planning to shoot the guy who has been hanging out with his girlfriend. Pastor, you've got to do something right now."

I quickly found Phil who looked angry, dangerous and ready to explode. I asked him if he had a gun with him.

When he said that he did, I told him that he needed to leave. That was the last time that I saw Phil before this dark night on April 10, 2010.

Phil stared at me menacingly as he said, "Well, you know what I can do. I spent over twenty years in prison."

There was no question as to what Phil was saying. He was threatening me so that I would abandon my intention for Cathy and me to sleep in the empty room at our property in South Central Los Angeles. I thought of that song, "*Who Let the Dogs Out?*" I needed to be careful how I answered Phil, as he was more than an ugly face with bad breath.

How did I come to be in this dangerous confrontation with Phil?

Three years earlier I bought a unique property on 92nd Street in Los Angeles consisting of nine buildings with a total of 32 bedrooms. I believed God was going to use this property to set people free from addiction. I leased it to my long time friend, the founder and director of a sober living program, who agreed to pay me a fair monthly rental.

At the time we took possession of the property, we were overflowing with vision. This property would allow us to double the number of people that we would be able to get off the streets of LA and out of jail. The miracle of recovery was just a prayer (and a bed) away.

"I see a campus of people who want to have their lives changed by the power and presence of the Lord," I told my friend. "We can build a close-knit Christian community where God uses us to disciple people as they leave the power of darkness and walk as children of light."

Jim Jones (not his real name) and I shared a burden for the least, the lost and the lonely. I had already leased to him and his ministry entity a triplex and a twelve-unit apartment house.

Jim managed housing and the practical aspects of receiving people from jail and the streets while I had spiritual oversight of our church – Open Arms Christian Center.

My purchase of the unique property on 92nd Street was an opportunity to expand our mercy/evangelism ministry to the large and growing number of addicts in Los Angeles.

I used my business acumen and credit-worthiness to buy property and then lease it to Jim and his ministry. The next three years were torturous, as the monthly lease payments were always too little and too late. I found myself chasing my friend by phone for the agreed lease payments. It became a daily act of frustration and financial survival.

When I finally made contact, I was seduced by his promises of, "Money is coming. I have a contract. It should be coming through any day." Every month meant another $5,000 to $10,000 loss. Only the sale of our other businesses and buildings in Montana allowed us to absorb the heavy losses each month.

I was a neophyte in the land of "ghettonomics." I believed a man's word was his bond. We would rather die than lie. But in the ghettonomics of South Central Los Angeles I learned that words and promises meant little or nothing. They were merely a desire or intention. Mostly they were the prelude to the stall. "I will call you later" meant nothing. "I will see you tomorrow" meant nothing. "I am sending the money" meant nothing.

"My conflict is so great," I confided in my wife. "I want my trust to be fully and completely in the Lord and not in man. The scripture says that 'some trust in horses and some in chariots but I will trust in the name of the Lord.'"

Only my wife, Cathy, and faithful friend and church administrator, Kert, knew how I agonized.

"Am I the biggest fool that ever lived? When was enough, enough? I can't be a sucker if I do what the Lord tells me to do. I must move in faith and not in fear." I proclaimed repeatedly to Cathy and Kert.

"You are not the biggest sucker that ever lived, but when he dies you will be," Kert assured me.

Perhaps the biggest dilemma was suppressing my optimistic perspective that everything will work out.

"I look at the delay in receiving money as a test of my faith. We made a decision that we would never make a decision based on fear but only faith," I reiterated as much to myself as to whoever was listening.

"I can't be a sucker if I do what the Lord tells me to do."

My vision was to build a community of believers where we experienced daily the miracle of redemption in the lives of the least, the lost and the lonely. "I believe that God knows how much stress and stretching we can handle," I confided in Cathy. "God is never surprised. He said that He would never leave us nor forsake us."

I could not believe that somebody would deliberately lie to me. The vision of a miracle-working Christian community was dying with each broken promise. Finally, I called Jim and told him that we needed to get together ASAP. He said he would come the next day but he didn't. He rescheduled for the following day and showed up an hour late.

As we sat around our small kitchen table, I told Jim, "We are out of gas and out of money." This elicited more promises about money coming, a signed contract, etc. I had heard it all before and it always worked on me to delay any more direct action. But now we were D-O-N-E. We were out of gas, out of money and out of faith.

As I looked at my friend and co-laborer, I remembered all the dreams we had shared about building something that would change people for eternity. We had traveled together, participated in one another's daughter's weddings, and shared conversations and meals over the past dozen years. Now, all we had was a pile of bills, a list of broken promises and a dead vision.

"I can't do it any more. I am tired and broke," I exclaimed to Jim. "I am losing $10,000 a month. I can't do this without any help from anybody else. I need you to give me back my properties. It's time for me to go in a new direction," I concluded.

My friend looked at me as if I had slapped his face. "I will pray about it and get back to you," he said. In order to alleviate some of my financial pressure (or alleviate his guilt), he gave me a small amount of money to apply to the monthly lease payments.

"Let's pray," said my friend. As we took one another's hands and bowed our heads to pray, I wondered if this was the last time that we would do this. We hugged and he left.

Later we heard that he had told his leaders, "I will die before I let this 'white guy' take my property." When I confronted him about this statement, he denied that he ever said it even though two different people at the meeting told me the same thing.

I was so conflicted by this racial slur coming from a man who had been my best friend for ten years. When he was accused of fornication years before, I confronted him with the allegation and believed his denial. Others separated from him, but I believed that a single, unconfirmed accusation against an elder could not be accepted as truth. There needed to be two or more witnesses.

Now, I was the "white guy." My friend used to say that "God's favorite race is the human race." I loved that statement and accepted it as a part of my DNA.

At Open Arms (the church we founded in 2001), I often forget whether somebody is brown, black or white. I recall an animated argument with one of the ladies attending Open Arms concerning the skin color of a guy named "Tim" who was also attending Open Arms.

I was telling her about this white guy named "Tim." She was adamant that Tim was black and I was equally adamant that he was white. "I have had many conversations with him and I know he is white," I argued.

"I know what color he is. He's my boyfriend," retorted Brenda who later married Tim.

A day later, Brenda brought Tim to me. "Here he is, Pastor. Look. He is black just like me," she concluded.

I was astonished to think that I had been so long pastoring Open Arms and working with the people that God gave us that I could no longer even recall the skin color of our people.

I had even given myself the Indian name, "Black Man in White Body." God looks on the color of our hearts, not the superficial color of our skin.

If what I heard from my inside informants was true, my friend was done praying. He was planning on a battle. I had been a lawyer for over twenty-five years, but had given it up to pastor God's people.

I knew lawsuits were a lousy way to settle differences. Didn't the scripture say that brothers should not go to court against a brother? It's better to suffer loss than let the heathen judge us.

"What do you think I should do?" I wrote to a close pastor friend in England.

God looks on the color of our hearts, not the superficial color of our skin.

"I want to be obedient to scripture even if it means suffering loss. But this is complicated. I owe almost $2,000,000 and need to pay out close to $30,000 a month in mortgage payments," I wrote.

I felt it was economically imperative that I get the properties back and start receiving income to pay the banks. I thought of the scripture that says, "Take joyfully the spoiling of your goods."

My English pastor friend quickly wrote back that God did not want me to roll over and be taken to bankruptcy court. "Do whatever you need to do. Bring a lawsuit if that's what it's going to take to get your property back," counseled my English pastor. Other family and friends counseled the same.

In the past when I had represented a Christian in a dispute with another "Christian," I told my client that it was highly possible that the other person was not even a Christian. After all, Christians don't lie, cheat, steal, commit adultery and do other acts common to the unbeliever.

I contacted my son Dugan, the lawyer in the family, and said, "It doesn't look good for a simple, peaceful return of the property. We need to go forward on the basis that it is going to be a full-fledged lawsuit."

"Okay, Dad, I will get right on it. I don't know how he can justify holding on to the property when he is not paying you the monthly lease," commented Dugan.

"I think he has convinced himself that he owns the property. He is telling people that we were partners. In the past, he has introduced me to different people as his partner."

After several days, I was able to get my friend to come for a follow-up to my request that he give me back my property. As we sat together around my table, Jim received one phone call after another.

Somebody wanted permission to spend two dollars. I could see that my friend would rather have a two-dollar conversation than deal with real issues. I suggested between phone calls that he return the properties one at a time over the next three months.

The meeting ended with Jim making more promises to catch up on some of the lease money that was owed. "The clinic is in place and should be generating the money to get everything caught up just like I've been saying," concluded my friend.

“I can’t go on. We need money NOW,” I emphasized. It was clear that Jim was giving me the ghetto stall, so I handed him the three-day notice to pay or quit.

“What’s this?” asked Jim.

“This is the next step to getting my properties back. It says you need to pay the rent or surrender the properties,” I explained.

“If you don’t give me back the properties, I will have no choice but to bring a lawsuit. I don’t want to do this but I have no choice. We can’t wait any longer,” I said.

As my friend of twelve years took the papers and left, I was overwhelmed with sadness. I wanted the blessing promised in Psalm 133 when “brothers dwell together in unity.” Gone was the vision of living next door to one another building a spiritual hospital for the sick.

With no response during the three-day period to pay or surrender the premises, my son and his legal team prepared a lawsuit. The lawsuit included a petition asking the court to give me immediate possession of the property so that I could receive rental income to make the monthly mortgages. My soon-to-be ex-friend filed papers opposing the lawsuit and showed up on the day of hearing with an attorney.

While we were waiting for our case to be heard, I sat on a bench in the hallway of the courthouse talking with Jim.

“I know that the property is yours. Any fool knows that,” admitted Jim. “I can’t just give it to you as I don’t have any place to take my people.”

We agreed that I would write something up and we would sign it and take it out of the court system. The court refused to grant the TRO (temporary restraining order), concluding that we had ample remedies by bringing another lawsuit for eviction.

This small, unexpected temporary victory must have given Jim a change of mind because he did not even respond to the letter I drafted attempting to settle our differences based on our conversation in the hallway of the courthouse.

I hired a well-known Los Angeles lawyer who advertised himself as “the King of Evictions.” After paying him over $5,000, he quickly prepared two lawsuits.

“Nothing will be quick and easy. It will take between 45 and 60 days to get your property back,” said the lawyer.

It was then that I had to wrestle with dark emotions of anger and bitterness. “I have done nothing but give and serve my friend for over ten years. I have raised thousands of dollars and given more money to him and his non-profit organization than anybody else. I can’t believe he is doing this to me,” I complained to Cathy, Kert and whoever else was around to listen.

It was during this time that I heard about an open, unoccupied room in what was called the “House of Genesis.” I thought we should make a run at re-taking possession of our property by simply moving into the unoccupied room in the House of Genesis on 92nd Street.

The lawsuit was high-centered with legalese and unacceptable delays. We had too many promises and not enough action. At the time, Cathy and I were living in a small apartment above our store-front church in South Central. Most of our furniture was stored in a storage unit. The lawsuits were languishing in the court system, the bills were mounting and nothing was really being resolved.

As I was praying, I felt God give me a strategy that would break the logjam. The strategy was simple - go to our storage unit and get a bed and some other furniture and move into the unoccupied room. It would require courage and boldness to do this.

"The last thing he wants is for me to be on the property," I pointed out. "Most of the folks really know and love us. We don't want to steal his people. They really are not his people or my people but God's people. We just need to press him to make the move sooner than later," I explained to the friends that were dumbfounded when they heard of my plan.

This was meant to put pressure on Jim, as the last thing he would want is me living on my own property with all the people that he wanted to stop me from relating to.

I felt God give me a strategy that would break the logjam.

He was more than upset. As we began unloading our U-Haul truck, all Jim's big gun administrative people came running. "Don't you move anything into that house," they screamed.

"If you move anything for Pastor Doug, you will be terminated and go back to jail," they told my friends who were helping us unload the U-Haul.

"Don't worry about it. Do what they say. We will get the furniture into the house," I told those helping us. The workers quietly sneaked away like they had stolen something. Almost immediately some good friends and former clients of the ministry, Eddie and Felicia Morgain, showed up to help us unload.

"Hey, Eddie! You and Felicia need to get off this property now," ordered big Ernest (Jim's manager of the 92nd Street campus for his ministry).

"I own the property and you can stay as long as you want," I told Eddie and Felicia.

"You heard the pastor. I'm not going anywhere. I'm going to help him unload and settle in," said Eddie. "I came to help the pastor and I'm going to help him get unloaded. This is his property."

Big Ernest placed his six foot three inches and 300 pounds right in front of the door. "I know you own this property but we have a lease. I'm going to call the police and tell them you are trespassing," said big Ernest.

"Go ahead and call the police. I have a right to come on my property whenever I want and to invite whoever I want to come with me," I told Ernest.

Along with two more of Jim's heathen henchmen, Ernest called the police and asked for them to come remove us from the property. It wasn't long before two policemen showed up.

They told the police that I was trespassing. "I own the property and have a right to come on the property whenever I want to," I explained to the officers.

"Our boss, Jim Jones has a lease on the property," said Ernest.

I explained, "There is nothing in the lease that prohibits me from living on my own property."

Big Ernest told the officers that the people living in the house did not want us in the house. "That's not true. I know these guys. I have been their pastor and friend," I stated.

Philip (the gun man who had already threatened me) spoke up, "I don't want him in the house." I told the officers that Philip did not even live in the House of Genesis but in the House of Revelation.

"Is that true?" demanded the policeman.

Big Ernest said, "He's in the process of moving into the House of Genesis tonight."

The policemen were not born last night and did not give any credence to Philip and Ernest. They called the guys over who actually lived in the house and asked if they minded our moving in. When they said "no problem," the police said it was a non-issue and left.

Philip's countenance had not changed much with all the interaction. I began making small talk with Philip about what he was doing and what was going on in his life as we were busy trying to assemble a bed frame for us to sleep on. "Here let me help you do that," said Philip as he tried to assemble the rebellious bed frame.

I sensed a small miracle and was reminded that "a soft tongue breaks the bone." If we hold our peace, the Lord will fight our battles.

How did a former lawyer, businessman and political candidate end up lying on a mattress on the floor in a drug and alcohol program in South Central LA?

The frame appeared to be missing a part so we gave up and just set the box springs and mattress on the floor. We put a sheet over the window and lay down to sleep with our clothes on. I thought of the soldiers who slept with their boots on so that they were ready for whatever they needed to do. Even though I was physically and emotionally spent with all the moving and confrontation, I could not sleep.

How did a former lawyer, businessman and political candidate end up lying on a mattress on the floor in a drug and alcohol program in South Central Los Angeles?

2

Counting the Gold

Position for Blessing - Do Whatever It Takes

As I LAY ON THE FLOOR next to my best friend and partner for life, praying for sleep, I considered the many changes that had come in my life since being labeled the most controversial student.

Just thirteen years earlier, life was totally different. We lived in Montana where I was a successful lawyer, pastor, and businessman. I was a big fish in a small pond. Over the years, I gained a reputation for representing many of the folks that nobody else wanted.

One client believed it was his constitutional right to drive a car without a driver's license. This client had been locked up many times for his unwillingness to go get a license. He was fine so long as he stayed on his own property, but when he drove on a county road or state highway he got arrested.

Jack Gehring was an eccentric who lived to fight big government when he was not tending to his buffalo ranch. "I need your help. I've been arrested for driving without a license. I want to fight it. Will you help me?" asked Jack.

One client believed it was his constitutional right to drive a car without a driver's license.

I told him that he should just get a driver's license and forget it. "It's bigger than that. I am standing up for all the people who won't fight for their rights," responded Jack.

I told Jack that it takes money to fight for these issues and that he was going to be found guilty of driving without a license. "How much will you charge me to take my case?" asked Jack.

"It's going to cost you $1,000 for me to go and lose your case in justice court," I told him. "I don't have the money, but I will let you shoot one of my buffalos," said Jack.

Now, I have never been a super big hunter, but the idea of hunting a buffalo appealed to my primal instinct, so I said, "You've got a deal."

Everything happened just the way I predicted. We went to court and made our constitutional argument to a bored Justice of the Peace.

He waited a nano-second before banging his gavel and saying, "I find you, Jack Gehring, guilty of driving without a license which is contrary to the laws of the State of

Montana and hereby sentence you to time served with the admonition that you are to either get a valid license or stay off all state, county and municipal roadways." I mumbled my thanks to the judge and left the courtroom ready to shoot a buffalo.

I took my twelve-year-old son with me as we drove to the Gehring buffalo ranch for the unique experience of shooting a buffalo. I brought my 30.06 hunting rifle given to me by my dad.

It did not have its own name like my dad's hunting rifle – "old meat in the pot," but it worked well enough to bag a few deer and antelope that we ground into sausage.

Real hunters have mocked me when I tell them about my great buffalo hunt.

Jack volunteered to shoot the buffalo for me. "Heck no! Shooting the buffalo is part of the deal. I don't just want the meat," I assured Jack.

"Well, you can't shoot the big ones. You need to shoot one of the smaller ones. The meat will be better than the big ones anyway," said Jack.

Real hunters have mocked me when I tell them about my great buffalo hunt. Just because the buffalo was fenced in did not diminish my excitement. We drove within fifty to seventy-five yards of the small herd.

"Now remember, don't shoot the big ones with horns. Which one are you looking at?" asked Jack. "I have that small one in my sight," I told him.

"Good. That's a two-year-old. He will be real good eating," Jack assured me. BANG!!!!!! The sound of the gun, the recoil and the two-year-old going down all seemed to happen at once. We drove up to the dying buffalo with the mobile butcher truck that I had contracted to come and field dress the kill, skin it and preserve the meat.

I took the buffalo hide to a local taxidermist to send away and get tanned so that I could make my own buffalo coat. The taxidermist ended up losing or selling my buffalo hide, so the jacket was a no-go. I am still dealing with a bit of anger and disappointment on that issue twenty-plus years later.

Jack was just one of the interesting clients that God gave me over a period of 25 years of practicing the law.

As I lay on the floor of the House of Genesis waiting for the sun to rise, I continued to think of God's leading in my life.

Not too long ago, I was the Republican candidate for Attorney General of Montana. Lawyering in Montana and pastoring in South Central Los Angeles had absolutely nothing in common.

My overactive, sleepless mind recalled another interesting case from my days as a Montana lawyer. It began when a friend that I knew through the local Full Gospel Businessmen's Fellowship called for my help.

"I need your help, Doug. My wife has insisted that I get some legal help or she is going to leave me," claimed Jack. (Yes, his name was also Jack.) Jack was well known for his controversial protests and his letters to the editor of our local newspaper. He seemed to be harmless in his political persuasions and activities.

"What happened? Why do you need a lawyer?" I asked Jack.

"The federal government has charged me with obstruction of justice for arresting the United States Attorney for crimes against the citizens of Montana," said Jack.

"How did you arrest him?" I asked.

"Well, I recorded a Citizen's Arrest Warrant at the County Clerk and Recorder's office where it was filed in the miscellaneous documents file," explained Jack.

The deputy Assistant US Attorney handling the matter was a friend of mine, as we had both been county attorneys in Eastern Montana. "What do I need to do to get rid of this thing?" I asked my friend.

"I know it's a waste of time for all of us. However, the U.S. Attorney wants to send a message to all of the crackpots that they cannot just file crazy papers arresting him or anybody else. I think we are going to have to let the judge deal with this," concluded my friend.

After hanging up, I felt inspired. If Jack had arrested the U.S. Attorney, he could un-arrest him. I prepared a legal-sounding document called "Withdrawal of Arrest Warrant," and had my client sign it.

We took the newly minted and signed document to the County Clerk and Recorder and had it recorded next to the arrest warrant. It seemed reasonable that if Jack had the power to make a citizen's arrest, he also had the power to un-arrest him.

A few days later I was standing in a Federal Courtroom before a very irate Federal District Court Judge. "Who prepared this document called Withdrawal of Arrest Warrant?" asked the judge angrily.

"I did your honor. It seemed clear to me that if my client had the power to arrest, he certainly had the power to un-arrest," I explained.

"I have a good mind to turn you over to the Lawyer's Bar Committee for unprofessional conduct. This is a travesty. You can't just prepare papers out of thin air and file them with the Clerk and Recorder," scolded the judge.

"Your honor, I was cleaning up a mess. Without my involvement, you and the U.S. Attorney's office would be looking at a lot more arrest warrants and other papers prepared by my client representing himself pro se," I explained.

Notwithstanding my strong and well-reasoned argument, the court was angry. "You have done nothing to solve this case. You are cluttering up the court system with this crazy case. If you do this again, I will cite you for contempt and report you to the Bar Committee for unprofessional conduct," intoned the judge.

"I have a good mind to turn you over to the Lawyer's Bar Committee for unprofessional conduct."

Afterwards I met with my friend from the U.S. Attorney's office. "Doug, I am sorry about that. I thought your attempt to solve the matter was fairly ingenious. I think my boss is willing to dismiss this matter if your client agrees that he is not going to do anything like this again."

"Sold! My client will sign or I will fire him and his wife of forty years will divorce him. This whole matter has caused way too much stress in their marriage. You prepare what you want him to sign and we will get it done," I assured him.

My client protested but he was tired and knew that his wife would kill him if he did not get this matter done with once and for all. It's wonderful to have clients with strong convictions. It is even more wonderful when they have the money to protect, defend and litigate their strong principles and convictions.

Although my law practice consisted of real estate, contracts, corporations, probate, divorce, personal injury and a smattering of civil and criminal litigation, I enjoyed the ones who danced to the sound of their own music (and had the money to pay me as they went through the system).

I remember receiving a call from a client named Verne who asked me to represent him in Federal Court on a charge of tax evasion. Verne had sold a gold mine for over two million dollars and placed the proceeds offshore. He believed that his "constitutional trust" was a proper tax shelter that allowed him to avoid the payment of any income taxes.

The IRS disagreed and had the U.S. Attorney file criminal charges against Verne and his wife Lorraine that could cause them to spend the rest of their lives in prison. The government argued that the constitutional trust was nothing but a fraudulent transaction intended to defraud the government.

Like most "conviction clients," Verne was not easy to manage. By the time that he called me he had already gone through several attorneys.

"Why are you calling me, Verne? There are many good lawyers who know a whole lot more about this area of law than I do. As you know, I am primarily a pastor and that takes the bulk of my time. I only do a little bit of legal work to help supplement my income," I explained.

"I know you. Jack told me how well you had represented him. You have a relationship with the U.S. Attorney and might get them to quit persecuting me. Besides, I know that you are honest and will always tell me the truth," responded Verne.

"I appreciate the recommendation of Jack but he had a totally different type of case. The charges against you and Lorraine are really serious. Unless we can negotiate a deal with the U.S. Attorney, you are going to end up in prison." I pointed out to him.

"Exactly! Again, this is why we need you. I have been praying for God to direct me and I believe He has directed me to you. Just take a look at it. I am not asking you to do it for nothing. I have money or I should say gold. I will pay you in gold," said the man who refused to take no for an answer.

I don't know whether it was the promise of gold or the strangeness of the case or the eccentricity of the client that made me want to take a good, long look at the case. "Alright, I will meet you and look everything over," I promised.

"Unless we can negotiate a deal with the U.S. Attorney, you are going to end up in prison."

After fifteen to twenty hours of going over all the documents, it was clear that the government had an airtight case. "Verne, you are not going to win. You should have just paid the taxes. Now you owe penalty and interest. You and your wife are at high risk of going to prison," I advised him.

Verne was an unhappy client but agreed to let me explore a possible plea bargain with the U.S. Attorney. Many back-and-forth calls and communications led us to the best offer that the government was willing to extend to us.

"I know you are not going to like it, Verne. You are going to pay two million dollars to the government but neither you nor Lorraine (his wife) will end up in jail. I don't think you are going to get a better deal."

"I don't like it," said Verne. "Let's get a delay on the trial date so that I can think about it."

"I will make the motion but it's highly unlikely that the court will move the trial date. I will file the motion for continuance tomorrow."

It took the Court very little time to dispose of my motion for continuance the next day in court.

My client has 'inadequate and incompetent' legal representation.

"Mr. Kelley, I have read your motion for continuance and the attached affidavit. I find it insufficient to move the court's discretion and grant your request. Motion denied. Do you have anything further, Mr. Kelley," asked the judge.

"Yes, your Honor. I did not include it in the affidavit but would ask the court to grant a continuance as my client has 'inadequate and incompetent legal representation.' I have never tried this type of case and for me to proceed to trial would be a classic case of incompetent counsel," I argued.

"I thought that I had heard everything but this takes the cake. I have never heard a lawyer argue that his representation was inadequate and reversible error. I am acquainted with your legal abilities and your experience and find your argument fallacious. If you persist in this argument, I will appoint a public defender to second chair your defense. In short, Mr. Kelley, you are competent and your motion for delay based upon incompetent counsel is hereby denied," ruled the judge.

I turned to my client and said, "Well, I had better get ready for trial. If you want to change horses in the middle of the stream, you better do it soon as the trial date is set."

"I have contacted a high powered criminal defense lawyer in Washington DC to look at this for me. I think we need to visit with him before deciding," Verne shared.

"No problem. I will be glad to send him whatever papers and answer whatever questions he might have."

About two weeks later, I found myself in the law office of one of the attorneys who represented those who broke into the Watergate Hotel under the direction of CREEP (Committee to Re-elect the President). "I have looked over the file, talked to the US Attorney handling the case and with your attorney," stated the criminal specialist.

I will remember that moment for the rest of my life.

"I am convinced that Doug has properly assessed the case and that the proposed settlement that he has in place is not going to be improved by our undertaking to represent you. I think you need to bite the bullet and do the deal. If something falls apart, we will be glad to come on board," concluded the attorney.

We flew back to Montana, signed the deal and received a dismissal of all charges against Verne's wife, Lorraine, and the deferred sentence on Verne. "Let's celebrate by going out for lobster or whatever you want," said Verne.

After a nice dinner of steak and lobster, we went out to Verne's car for the payment of my legal bill of $10,000. I will remember that moment for the rest of my life.

My client did not put money in the bank or use checking accounts the way normal people did. He paid me in one ounce Canadian Maple Leaf gold coins. I will never forget the gold lighting up the inside of Verne's car as he counted out all the gold coins.

Life is a journey full of cuts and scrapes, highs and lows, successes and failure.

As I lay on the floor of the Genesis House in South Central Los Angeles, my mind wanted to go to happier days. I wanted to think about receiving all those gold coins. One of the keys to being blessed is focusing on past victories or happy times when God was near.

David understood this principle of positioning when he answered those who thought it impossible for him to defeat Goliath. David told his critics:

"Your servant has killed both the lion and the bear; this uncircumcised Philistine shall be like one of them, because he has defiled the armies of the Living God. The Lord who rescued me from the paw of the lion and the paw of the bear will rescue me from the hand of this Philistine" (1 Sam 17:36-37).

David knew that during a time of severe testing, a key to being blessed was remembering past victories. Life is a journey full of cuts and scrapes, highs and lows, successes and failure. God's blessing comes to you and me just like it did to David as we do whatever He puts in front of us. For David, he dealt with a bear and lion in preparation to deal with Goliath. For me, I dealt with two Jacks and a Verne in preparation to be blessed.

In the midst of doing what is before us, we are not always aware that it is preparation for something greater. Blessing comes as we faithfully do the little things.

This book is about finding His blessing whether you are laying on a floor in South Central Los Angeles or counting gold coins in Montana.

3

"Authority is Like Underwear"

Position for Blessing - Come Under Authority

I HAVE BEEN CALLED to minister in South Central Los Angeles among the "unblessed." Most of them have nothing. They have a past filled with bad decisions, rebellion, prison, sickness, addiction, lying and betrayal.

Our church is called Open Arms and it is open to whosoever God sends to us. Our mission is to "give hope and help to the brokenhearted." The brokenhearted come burned, beaten and broken by life. Some want a small respite from the street or prison while others really want to make a permanent change.

"Everybody is either blessed or unblessed. It's all about coming under God's authority," I preached to the recovering addicts at Open Arms House of Hope.

Many of the blessed attribute our being blessed to simply doing what we were told. Instead of rebelling against our parents, we did what they said. We went to college. We delayed getting a job, buying a car, getting into a serious relationship, or taking the other detours and distractions that delayed God's blessing.

Open Arms is in the business of nursing the brokenhearted with the Word of God until they are strong enough to walk hand in hand with the Lord. We are a hospital with not enough doctors and nurses able to minister to the needs of those coming out of prison and off the streets. For them to ever walk a life of meaning and purpose, they need to COME UNDER AUTHORITY.

Our mission is "to give hope and help to the brokenhearted."

My wife Cathy and I have taught a Parenting Seminar all over the world. It's called "Who's in Control?" The greatest chance to receive God's blessing is to let God, through parents, have control of your life until you are mature and responsible enough to make good decisions.

There are many authorities in life but none is bigger than the authority of God. Just like the rich man who failed to come under authority, the men and women who come to Open Arms need to discover the authority of the Lord.

At the heart of Christianity is the issue of authority. Man is born with SELF as the authority. Even babies are all about "me, me, me." They want what they want NOW. I was invited to come to Christ many times before I finally responded. I delayed my decision to receive Jesus as my Savior because I inherently knew that coming to Christ would change my life.

The Bible says we go from darkness to light. We go from children of the Devil to children of God - from damned to saved, from Hell to Heaven, from self-deciding and deceiving to God-directing and influencing. I wasn't sure that I wanted to give up the Doug that I had grown to know and love for the Doug that would be changed by Jesus.

In September, 1970, I had had enough of the old man – his motivations, manipulations and maneuverings. I yielded to the pressure of my brother Don and Bob Malberg, my next-door neighbor from childhood, who pressed me to come to a Bible study.

"Get up. We are going to church and you need to come with us," pleaded my brother.

"No way! I was out until early this morning. I'm shot and hung over from drinking too much. I am hearing drums in my head. Let me go back to sleep," I said.

"We are not leaving unless you agree to go to church with us tonight," they insisted.

"Okay. If you leave right now, I'll go with you tonight," I conceded.

Later when I woke up, I remembered my promise to go to the church meeting. However, I did not tell them that I would go sober. With more doubt than faith, I went and drank enough beer to encourage my brother and friend to withdraw the invitation to the church service.

"Are you ready to go?" asked my brother.

"You sure that you want me to go with you? I've been out drinking a bit," I slurred.

"No problem. You'll fit right in."

My drunkenness did not appear to be the deal breaker that I was expecting. Therefore, my Hemmingway code of ethics compelled me to honor my word.

At the meeting there were fifty or sixty people singing and clapping. I joined in, thinking that I was at a Shakey's Pizza Parlor. Soon the music was over and it was time to have the Bible study. They were going through Chapter 10 of First Corinthians. As I was about to nod off from the effect of too much beer, they read 1 Corinthians 10:13:

> "There is no temptation taken you but such as is common to man, but God will not permit you to be tempted above that which you are able but will with the temptation provide a means of escape that you may be able to bear it."

I sobered up instantly and found my eyes glued to the scripture. At the end of the meeting, Creed Davis, the pastor, came over to me and asked if I had any questions.

"What does this scripture mean?" I asked the Pastor.

"It means that God knows what you are going through. It means that he has a special plan to get you through whatever pain or problem you are experiencing. God's plan is simple and uncomplicated. He takes our sins and gives us His forgiveness. The only way to escape Hell and eternal judgment is to repent of your sins and invite Jesus Christ to come into your life," he explained to me.

"But how do I know that I can believe the Bible is the Word of God?" I asked. I really needed to know because I was the mocker and scoffer who just the week before had made fun of a Charismatic Catholic plumber that I worked with.

The pastor patiently shared an unbelievable story about scientists needing to use the Bible to compute for some missing time.

"The best evidence that the Bible is true is that it is totally consistent. However, the scientists at NASA had to go to the Bible to account for missing time as they were planning the flight plan of a satellite. They had to put into the computer the fact that God turned back the sun. Once they did this, they were able to account for a missing day," stated the pastor.

I went from being my own authority to coming under God's authority. The devil was stunned.

After a few more meaningless (and forgettable) questions meant to salvage my agnostic pride, I went forward and sat in a chair in the middle of the room and prayed to receive Christ as my Lord and Savior. I now had a new authority in my life.

The legal, spiritual transaction was over in seconds. I went from darkness to light. I went from being my own authority to coming under God's authority. The devil was stunned. For years the devil had me doing his will, walking in his plan for my life, yielding to his authority.

Even some of the saints were stunned. The pastor's wife later confided in me that she was distraught when she heard, "Doug Kelley is coming to the Sunday night meeting." My reputation for controversy had gone before me and she was concerned that the college debater would become a meeting disrupter. Little did she know that it was my time to come under the authority of the Lord Jesus Christ.

Not too long ago I was preaching on a Sunday morning when I was interrupted by an intoxicated man waving a beer can and asking, “Where are the doughnuts?”

I told the ushers to get him a doughnut and find him a seat.

When the man did not come back into the church service, I asked the usher what happened to our unexpected visitor. The usher said that the man was concerned about his beer.

I told the usher that we should have put his beer into the church refrigerator and given it to him at the end of the service. After all, I know that God saves drunks. God is in the “whosoever will business.”

Most of our folks have a difficult time understanding the grace and love of God. A lady known as the neighborhood drunk has come dancing down the aisle at Open Arms several times on a Sunday morning. She is always met with love and grace as we try to introduce her to the only authority that will change her life and set her free from drugs and alcohol.

In my time as a lawyer and debater, I have always sought to find the authority in a person’s life. I cannot go into a court of law with only my opinion. The judge (aka “the court”) wants to know where it is written. He will ask, “What is your authority?” Oftentimes, lawyers give the court a memo of authorities outlining the basis for their argument.

It's been said that if a lawyer has the law on his side, he pounds on the law. If he has the facts, he pounds on the facts. If he has neither the law nor the facts, the lawyer pounds on the table.

The law of authority is especially true when it comes to science. We have the law of gravity that is the dominant authority. What goes up must come down. However, the law of lift can overcome the law of gravity for a season. Understanding authority is a key to being successful.

Several years ago I was preparing to preach on a Sunday morning and then lead a team of 22 people on a short term mission to the Philippines. I was praying about what relevant and timely message God wanted spoken to our church when these words came to my mind, "AUTHORITY IS LIKE UNDERWEAR."

Whenever a man tells his wife that she needs to submit, he is wearing his underwear on the outside.

I thought this to be a strange revelation, befitting my controversial label.

When I asked the Lord what this strange message meant, He reminded me that true authority is not flaunted as some external garment. Authority has a definitive purpose but it is not for show and tell.

I shared this teaching revelation with a men's group at my brother's church in Missoula, Montana. I even brought a pair of underwear to the meeting. I did not have the courage to wear them on the outside of my pants which would be a more graphic statement of what not to do.

I explained to the men that many of them were guilty of wearing their underwear on the outside of their jeans. Whenever a man tells his wife that she needs to submit, he is wearing his underwear on the outside. God wants mutual submission (Eph 5:21). If men will submit to the needs of their wives, their wives will joyfully submit to their authority.

All authority is delegated and limited (except for God). Authority should never be our goal. If we want to be great (or have authority), we need to become the servant of all. Jesus said that He did not come to be served but to serve. Jesus said that what He did we should do also.

Too many want to "Lord it over others." In God's church nobody should govern (have authority over others) unless they are involved in getting their hands dirty through shepherding. In their excellent little book on shepherding, Dr. Kevin Leman and William Pentak argue that "when directing your people, use persuasion, not coercion."

Watchman Nee said that whenever you come to a new place, your primary task is to find the authority and submit yourself to that authority. Nee believed God provides protection to those who come under authority. This is why God admonishes us to obey those in authority, pray for those in authority and give honor to whom honor is due (Heb 13:7).

We have seen many political and spiritual leaders abuse the authority with which they have been entrusted. They forget that their purpose is to serve those within their sphere. Cults produce leaders like Jim Jones who on November 18, 1978 led 913 of his followers in Jonestown, Guyana to drink cyanide-laced Kool-Aid. Many Christians have forgotten that they serve at the pleasure of the King.

When I was getting my Bachelor of Arts degree in Political Science, I learned that a benevolent despot (aka monarch) heads the best form of government. The monarch serves for the benefit of his subjects.

The Kingdom of God has a King named Jesus who has made a way for all of His subjects to come into a relationship with the Father. The opposite of a monarchy is a dictatorship. A dictator does not serve for the benefit of his subjects but only for himself.

Many Christians drop out of church when they come into contact with a dictator attempting to control their lives. A wise man seeks counsel but a fool just goes down the road to do whatever he wants to do.

Within the church, we have both types of leaders wielding authority in the name of the Lord. Wolves in sheep's clothing need to be marked and avoided. Jesus is the Good Shepherd and He has many committed, loving and caring under-shepherds to do His will.

During the 1970s, the "shepherding movement" arose. The essence of this movement dealt with the issue of authority. At the core of the movement was the doctrine that "every man needs a pastor."

The question was not one of relational accountability as much as it was one of hierarchical systematization. Churches were split by this teaching; families were hurt; and many Christians were deceived and disillusioned.

In the mid-1980s, I was picked up at an airport by a very inquisitive driver who was escorting me to my speaking engagement.

With very little preliminary conversation, my new friend asked, "Who is your pastor?"

"All mature Christians should be directly shepherded by Jesus Christ. The real issue is accountability. Although I am shepherded by Jesus Christ, I am accountable to my wife and many others," I explained to my interrogator.

A man who is not accountable is a danger to himself and others. Accountability is connected to the whole issue of authority. I am accountable first to the Lord, next to my wife and family, then to the elders of the local church and other leaders that God has put in my life. There is tremendous protection in having people who love you enough to speak truth into your life.

I am alarmed by those who tell me their pastor lives hundreds or thousands of miles away (sometimes in another country). They say this as if it gives them a sense of legitimacy but the opposite is true. The Bible says, "Better is a neighbor that is near than a brother far off" (Prov 27:10).

Many are quick to put everybody in a pecking order and obey completely the orders of those over them. This is similar to the papal system of priests, bishops, archbishops, cardinals and pope. They sing the song *Trust and Obey* and drink the Jim Jones doctrinal Kool-Aid without challenging those in authority.

A man who is not accountable is a danger to himself and others.

Paul failed to get that revelation when he withstood Peter to his face over Peter succumbing to the legalism of the Judaizers in Galatia. Paul did not go aside for a private chat but challenged Peter in a public manner. May God give us the wisdom and courage of Paul, willing to confront wrong-headed authority coming with false and dangerous doctrine (Gal 2:11-21).

There are three primary types of authority. The most common authority is the "authority of position." The one with the label (pastor, elder, deacon, Senator, Mayor, business owner, etc.) has the authority. We recognize their authority and submit and support them accordingly.

Another authority is the "authority of personality." Many people come on so strong that we tend to defer to Mr. or Mrs. Type A. Psychologists have identified an aggressive, take-charge type of personality as a Type A person.

Obviously, the environment gets a bit dicey when two Type A personalities are in the same room making their case for the decision.

I went on a short-term mission trip with another Type A (yes, I am one too), and it was obvious early on that we would have no peace unless I let him make decisions. I hate to admit that I played the role of sniper and shot at as many flawed decisions as possible.

If you want to be blessed, you need to position yourself for blessing.

The last type of authority is the "authority of knowledge." This is my favorite since it recognizes what a person knows more than his label or personality. If we have a plumbing problem, let the plumber move in his authority. If we have a spiritual problem, we let those who have expertise or anointing in that area move in their anointing. It's good to defer to those who truly know what they are doing.

Remember, if you want to be blessed, you need to position yourself for blessing. The Bible says if you walk with fools you become a fool. If you walk with wise men, you become wise. God wants to bless you.

In law, I learned that a gift had three parts – donative intent, delivery and acceptance. God has made His intent clear. He wants to give good things to His children. We need to get in a position so that He can complete the delivery and we can accept the gift.

If you submit to His authority by accepting Him as Lord and Savior, you are on your way to being blessed. There are many principles that we need to be aware of and obedient to if we are going to receive His blessing. Even after forty-five years of walking with the Lord, I am still finding principles and nuances of principles that help me receive His blessing.

An old song challenged everybody to "get under the spout where the glory comes out." In Mathew 8:5-13 a centurion positioned himself and his family to receive blessing. He recognized Jesus' authority, made a request of the authority and received the benefit of the authority. Jesus did not talk about authority but complimented the centurion for his faith. Jesus said, "I have not found such faith in Israel."

The purpose of all legitimate government is to bring protection and order.

People who fail to come under authority are in prison, broke, confused, sick and angry. Those who come under authority are like the centurion – safe, secure and blessed.

When I first graduated from law school, I moved to a small town in eastern Montana. The people were self-sufficient and generally had a hatred for government. They wanted to be left alone without the heavy hand of government.

Out of this anti-government movement came a group called the "Freemen." They opposed all government except for the local sheriff. Their anti-government position appealed to anti-government people all over the United States. They ended up in a standoff with the federal government that lasted for a couple of months.

The Christian is not anti-government, for government is on His shoulders (Is 9:8). The kingdom of God is all about government and authority. The purpose of all legitimate government is to bring protection and order. To be a true "freeman" we need to receive the grace, love, mercy and salvation that come only from a relationship with Jesus Christ.

As previously stated, everybody experiences Heaven and Hell. We are blessed when we experience Heaven on earth. We are unblessed when we suffer deprivation, sickness or loss. We can call this Hell on earth.

As an urban missionary in South Central Los Angeles, I am a white guy living among black and brown people in an environment of alcohol, drugs, guns and poverty. They have their own unique value system and speak their own language.

One of the new phrases that I have learned is a prison term called "ear hustling." It means you are listening in on a conversation that is going on near you. Well, if you are going to position yourself for a blessing, you need to ear hustle as we discuss relevant Biblical principles that will position you for a blessing. The Bible says "Let those who have an ear hear.

4

Dead Men Don't Despair

Position for Blessing - Die to Self

Wisdom says if we fail to learn the lesson of history, it is bound to be repeated. How many times have we walked around certain mountains (or problems) because we have been too stubborn to admit that we were wrong or too proud to ask for help? We are like a man driving in circles without a GPS, map or a clue on what street to take.

As I preached the last sermon of 2010, I looked out over my congregation of former drug dealers, prostitutes, criminals and addicts and announced with unwavering conviction, "It's been a Hell of a year." The gasps were visible from the front to the back of our small sanctuary.

"I know. Many of you are troubled that I have used the word 'Hell'. If this offends you, great! Hell is just as real as this church building or you and me," I announced.

"Most of you are religious and would never use the word "Hell" inside the church but wait until you hit the street. Don't be blinded by a religious reaction to a Biblical word. Hell has its own lessons. Will you learn the lessons from Hell?" I asked rhetorically.

If we learn from spending time in Hell, we are able to position ourselves for blessing. God permits Hell on earth to teach us, grow us and ultimately bless us. God permitted Hell on earth for Job when he lifted His hand of protection from Job. He permitted Hell on earth for Lazarus and his sisters, Mary and Martha, when He allowed Lazarus to die.

Daily we get to decide between Heaven and Hell....

Although we are Heaven-bound and called to pray for "Heaven on earth," we are not immune from the tribulation, suffering and separation of Hell on earth.

Many Christians believe that Satan is in control of this world, as the Bible refers to him as the "god of this world." However, the Bible also says that the earth is the Lord's and the fullness thereof (Ps 24:1). He is the God of Heaven and earth (Deut 4:39).

"Daily we get to decide between Heaven and Hell by praying or not praying, by obedience or disobedience, by faith or no faith. We are like men and women in the gap (Ezek 22:30) with one foot firmly planted on earth and our other foot in either Heaven or Hell. Obedience brings Heaven while disobedience brings Hell," I explained.

Have you ever wondered why some "get it" and others don't? The "it" can be a job, a revelation or some other blessing. The Bible says that God's Word does not profit us unless it is mixed with faith (Heb 4:2).

Many years ago my wife and I decided that we would never make a decision based on fear. Faith and fear are directly opposite.

One of the lessons I learned in 2010 living through a time of Hell was DON'T BE OVERWHELMED BY DISAPPOINTMENT.

Many of us come to Christ expecting that we will live a problem-free life. We have found easy street. No more pressures, problems or setbacks. Life is good. God loves us. He will protect us and bless us.

While God loves us and wants to bless us, the way God blesses us is by using torment, suffering and separation to bring us to maturity.

My dad, Percy Webster Kelley, was a big Irishman who taught me the value of relationships. He had friends all over the world because he was the guy who would give you the shirt off his back. He was my hero and I wanted to be him when I grew up.

He was also a great communicator with friends for life. Even when somebody betrayed him, Dad was willing to forgive and re-establish relationship as though nothing had happened.

In the early 80s we pioneered a church in Helena, Montana. One of the faithful men helping build the church was a friend for ten years. I had found him cutting meat behind a butcher counter and saw his potential as a mighty man of God. We became best friends. He even named his firstborn son after me. I remember the day that our relationship changed.

I had been out hunting deer and returned in time to get ready for the midweek service. When I arrived home, Bud Dziekonski, affectionately known as the "big Pollack" from the Bronx, was parked in my driveway.

"What's up, big guy?" I asked as I unloaded my gear and moved as quickly as possible.

"I need to talk to you right now," stated Bud.

"I am really pressed to get ready for church. How about we visit later?" I asked.

"It can't wait. You do what you need to do and I will follow you around and tell you what's happening," insisted Bud.

As he followed me from room to room (even into my shower), Bud told me a story of betrayal that is as old as Absalom betraying his father King David.

"Joe (not his real name) is openly telling people that you are making bad decisions. He's telling the people that he is supposed to be the pastor of the church and that you need to step aside. If he isn't stopped, it's going to split the church right down the middle," concluded Bud.

I was shocked by these allegations and could not believe that my close, intimate friend of over ten years would do this to me. I thought Bud's report was probably nothing more than a misunderstanding.

"We will get the mid-week service started and then go to my office with Joe and visit about this. The Bible says if a brother is overtaken in a fault, we must confront them," I explained.

After the worship was over, I turned the teaching portion of the service over to the elder who was already scheduled to teach. Bud, Joe and I went to my office where I told Joe that Bud had something to say.

In a rendition of an Old Testament prophet ripping his own clothes as a prophetic statement, Bud grabbed the top of his own shirt and pulled downward while prophesying, "You have tried to tear this church apart even as this shirt has been torn apart but God says no more." As the buttons popped off Bud's shirt, Joe looked worried that the big fellow from the Bronx might physically assault him.

I was hoping that my friend Joe would say that there was a misunderstanding and give a reasonable explanation of the prophetic statement uttered by the Bronx bomber. However, he did not. Instead, Joe began to mumble justification for everything he said and talked about his ministry.

"You have no ministry in this church until we sort out this issue. What Bud has accused you of is very serious. You have been accused of being an Absalom," I explained.

Spiritual pride and stubbornness took over and the meeting ended without any repentance or reconciliation. Others attending the home meeting led by Joe quickly confirmed his "Absalom-like comments." One family left the church with my beloved brother.

I was brokenhearted by the whole betrayal. I found myself physically crying like David when he heard of the death of his son Absalom. Until that moment, I never understood David's heart for his deceiving, disloyal, disobedient son.

Also like David, I had faithful elders in the church to minister to me. I had thought that Joe was going to succeed me as pastor of the church. I had a big hole in my heart where Joe had lived for ten years.

I wish that I could give you a report that we subsequently reconciled and all was well in the Promised Land. I love happy endings but such is not always the case.

Joe (aka Absalom) ended up with his own church but could not hold on to it or his marriage. The last I knew he had gone through three more marriages. I still love him and I still have an empty place in my heart where he once lived. He was a gifted godly man that failed to come under authority, repent for his sins and be reconciled.

I loved being a pastor but felt the prophetic pull of God. In my prayer time in February, 1984, I heard the Lord call the church back into the marketplace.

"The church has become monastic and needs to go from the monastery to the marketplace," said the still, small voice of the Lord.

"The church has become monastic and needs to go from the monastery to the marketplace..."

"What does this mean? What are you saying, God? Are you telling me to go back into politics? Are you resurrecting my old dream of serving in government?" I asked the Lord.

I did not know what it meant to "go from the monastery to the marketplace" but thought that God was resurrecting my dream of being involved in politics.

When I came to Christ, I deliberately placed my Isaac (i.e. politics) on the altar in order to serve the Lord. I thought politics was my past and not my present or future. A good friend reminded me that God did not kill Isaac but gave him back to Abraham.

My decision to obey the Lord by taking the church into the marketplace was full of difficulties and unanswered questions. I had been a Christian for fourteen years and followed a simple theology of "trust and obey." He speaks and I do. He is the boss and I am his worker.

In February of 1984, after God had spoken to me about taking the church back to the marketplace, I asked God if I should run for Attorney General of Montana. The same, still, small voice that had directed me for fourteen years said, "You decide."

I didn't want to decide. I wanted to obey. Or maybe I just wanted somebody to blame if it did not work out right.

"As He is, so are we in this present world."

So, I asked my wife if I should run. She deferred and said simply, "You decide." I thought the elders, the deacons or the congregation would have a strong opinion, but as I went from one to the next to the next they each said YOU DECIDE. I wondered if this was even a Biblically correct doctrine. It sounded like heresy. What happened to "trust and obey?"

As I went to the scripture, God spoke to me. He said, "As He is, so are we in this present world." Jesus does not want us to just bide our time on planet earth until some day we get to Heaven. He wants us to "rule and reign" today.

Even the first message of Genesis to our great-, great-grandparents Adam and Eve was to take dominion. God grows us through trials and tribulations. Our Heavenly Father is busy pouring His spirit, Word and character into us. Just like an adult son or daughter, we receive the character and values of our parents and then need to take what we have learned to the highways and byways of life.

"But, God, I just want to obey you. I want you to tell me what to do. I promise that I will be a good soldier and do what you say," I argued in my prayer closet.

The Lord whispered, "You are mature enough to make the decision. You have my Word, my values and my character. It is time to be the man I have called you to be. Real men take responsibility for the decisions that they make. You are my man. Make the decision and I will bless you whether you run or don't run," whispered the Lord.

"Okay, Lord. But I am scared. Nobody is preaching this doctrine of 'you decide.' I don't want to be a heretic but I know your voice and I am going to get out of the boat and walk on the water," I said in silent surrender.

Too many Christians are reluctant to take responsibility for their own decisions. They want to have somebody to blame. They hide behind spiritual phrases like, "God showed me, God told me." We love the intimacy implied by closeting with God but He wants us to grow up and own our decisions.

Brother Lawrence, a 15th Century monk and author of the book *The Practice of the Presence of God*, understood this principle better than most of us. When something good happened, Brother Lawrence gave God all the credit and glory. However, if things went bad, he took the blame. May God free each of us from the heathen perspective of being a God-blamer.

Once the decision was made to run for Attorney General of Montana, I needed to transfer the pastorate of our church to someone else. I could think of nobody more called and gifted than my brother Don who was successfully pastoring a rural church in northern Montana.

After four years of pastoral ministry, our church in Helena, Montana had plateaued between 150 and 175 people. Almost simultaneous to the revelation of going "from the monastery to the marketplace," I asked the Lord why we seemed to have quit growing numerically. He spoke to me a threefold solution.

"For the church to grow you need a new building, a new name and a new pastor," instructed the Lord.

I was happy about the possibility of getting a new building, as our existing building was a former metal warehouse on a dirt road. It was not in a "customer friendly" area as one needed a guide dog or GPS to find it in the north Helena Valley. Even the new name was exciting. But the third condition left me wondering if I was suffering from revelation overload.

"Did I hear right? You want me to step down as the pastor?" I asked the Lord.

"For the church to grow you need a new building, a new name and a new pastor."

With quiet reassurance God reminded me that He had called me to a walk of faith. I could not receive His next gift unless I let go of the one that was now filling my hand and life.

I remembered an old saying, "Ours is not to reason why, ours is but to do and die." I was a soldier in the army of the Lord. The church did not belong to me but to Him. His name was on the door, not mine.

In an attempt to press my brother into coming to pastor the church, I called him on the phone and shared my "three-pronged revelation" on what needed to happen for the church to grow.

"I think it's God. He is ready to promote you. He wants to bring you in from the wilderness. Talk to Bev (his wife), pray and get back to me ASAP," I urged him.

I was confident that he was the man and that God was going to move him and release me so that I could concentrate on running for Attorney General of Montana. I needed to wait for almost a week before my brother called me with his decision.

"Well, we fasted and prayed for three days but do not have peace that this is the right time for us to move. We are still working hard to build some leaders but have nobody who could step in and take over if we left," concluded my brother.

I still believed that my brother was the right man for the job. Without a replacement I needed to do double duty as a pastor and candidate for Attorney General.

Every time my name appeared in the paper or was spoken on radio or television they referred to me as pastor/lawyer Doug Kelley. I called the Associated Press (AP) reporter who was a believer and personal friend and asked him to quit referring to me as a pastor.

"I am not running for chief Shepherd of Montana but Attorney General. The fact that I pastor a church is no more relevant to the election than the fact that you are a leader in another church is relevant to your duties as an AP reporter," I argued passionately.

"Sorry, Doug. I would do it if I could, but I have already been told by my boss that the thing that makes your race interesting is the fact that you are a pastor running for Attorney General. If I did not put it in, they would add it back and chew on me for omitting it," explained my Christian brother.

About two weeks after successfully winning the Republican primary for Attorney General (no opposition), I was praying when I sensed the "still, small voice of the Lord."

"You are going to lose and go to work for Pat Robertson's political organization -the Freedom Council," whispered that same familiar voice that just a few months earlier said, "You decide."

I shared this revelation with Cathy and two leadership couples from the church as we were spending a day out at a lake just east of Helena.

"What are you going to do? Are you going to just go through the motions or what?" they all asked.

"No. I intend to work even harder than I would without this revelation. It's imperative that if I lose it's because it's God's will. I don't want to lose because I am lazy or super-spiritual," I said.

"You are going to lose."

"What does that really mean?" they asked.

"It means that I intend to test the spirit to find out if God was really whispering in my ear. I will work even harder, raise more money and campaign 24/7 until the polls close on the first Tuesday in November."

God had given me a specific passage of scripture in Judges 19 when the Lord had told Israel to go to battle against the tribe of Benjamin. They went to war and lost. They quickly regrouped and asked God what they were supposed to do and the Lord told them to go to war a second time.

They went in obedience to the revelation that they received and lost again. This time the leaders fell on their face and cried out to God.

"What do you want us to do, Lord?" they cried out.

"Go again. This time you will win," said the Lord.

This story taught me that God is more concerned about obedience than winning and losing. God counts different than we do and works off a different time frame.

Subsequent to the revelation that I would "lose the election," we had a great need in our campaign for money. Money is called the "mother's milk of politics" and without it you will be nothing but another name on the ballot.

I wanted to live a life of excitement, measured risk and no regret.

It was time to pay for the billboards advertising "Doug Kelley - A Lawyer You Can Trust." Fundraising was very slow as most people thought that I was a long shot to unseat the present attorney general who was seeking his third term. Other races were vacuuming up all the campaign donations.

In every political race there is usually a finite amount of people willing to donate. Thus, donors are always looking at making the best use of their donor dollars. Nobody wants to bet on a loser whether at the horse track or the ballot box.

One of the guiding philosophies of my life is to "live with no regrets." When people die, they don't regret what they did but what they failed to do. I wanted to live a life of excitement, measured risk and no regret.

"We need to go to the bank and borrow $50,000 if we are going to do everything we can to win," I confided in my wife. I was hesitant to push the issue because I was still aware that God said I was going to lose the election. I could not spend what little equity we had in our home without Cathy being in agreement.

"I think we need to go see Dan Johnson at First National about loaning us the money we need to buy the billboards," said Cathy.

"Are you sure? It's likely that we will lose and never get our money back. If we give the bank a second mortgage on our home, it's possible that we will have to sell the house in order to pay the debt. Are you really ready to live in a trailer house?" I asked.

"We need to do everything we can to win. If that costs us our home, then so be it. I don't really want to live in a trailer but I want to do whatever it takes to finish what we have begun."

"We need to do everything we can to win. If that costs us our home, then so be it."

I could not believe that God had given me such a faithful life partner – willing to jump off the cliff with me even though God had spoken that we were going to lose. After we lost the election, I shared how impressed I was with Cathy's willingness to give up her home to follow the Lord.

"I did not even remember the word you got about losing. I was focused on doing what it took to live without regret. We always said that we did not want to reach the end of our life asking 'what if' or 'if only,'" concluded Cathy.

When I met with the banker and told him that I wanted to borrow money for my political campaign, he just shook his head and said, "This is not a good decision."

"You are not thinking straight. You don't want to borrow money and put it into a political campaign. You would be better to take the money to bet on the horses," said my banker.

"I hear what you are saying but we made a deep-seated philosophical decision that we are going to be the kind of people who live without regrets," I explained.

"How are you going to pay it back if we loan you the money?" asked the banker.

"We hope to win and pay it back with campaign donations," I said.

"And, if you do not win and do not have enough campaign donations, how will you pay it back?"

"Well, we are giving you a second mortgage on our home and we will sell it and pay back the bank from the proceeds of the sale."

"And, if the house doesn't sell, how will you pay back the bank?"

"If we do not have campaign contributions or proceeds from the sale of the house, I will go back to work as a lawyer and pay you from my legal business," I concluded.

It was then that I violated a basic leadership principle. I made a decision without talking with my elders or getting the benefit of wise, godly counsel. I told my banker that I would go back to practicing law.

He looked at me and said, "Okay but I still think it is a mistake to borrow money for a political campaign."

I am a bit foggy after all these years whether it was $50,000 or $60,000 that he loaned me but I am not confused about the end result. We ran a vigorous campaign supported by Christians, homeschoolers, business people and Republicans from all over the state.

Nevertheless, God was not mocked. On election night, the television commentators were talking to one another.

"Now we turn to an interesting race that pits long-term Attorney General Mike Greeley against pastor/lawyer Doug Kelley. We thought this might be the big surprise of the night with Kelley ousting Greely. But, it looks like all the buzz out on the street might have been a case of Kelley supporters talking to one another," concluded the commentator.

In politics, if you lose by 10% or more, you are soundly trounced. I think I was beaten 57% to 43%. Yeah, I got my spiritual clock cleaned. I will always be grateful to the 140,798 wonderful, spiritual and insightful Montana people who pulled the lever for me.

Just as God whispered in my ear five months earlier, I lost the election and went to work full time for Pat Robertson's political entity, The Freedom Council. I accepted the position as Northwest Regional Director of The Freedom Council, overseeing eleven states from Alaska to Minnesota.

My brother had a change of heart and sensed a green light from God. He packed up his wonderful wife and two daughters and moved to Helena, Montana to take over the church on July 1, 1985 while I traveled from Alaska to Minnesota recruiting political candidates and encouraging Christians to be salt and light, to occupy until Jesus came back for His Bride.

Twenty-two months later, my brother resigned and handed the church back to me. "I don't believe that I am supposed to pastor Mount Helena Community Church. I'm a tenant farmer working a farm that belongs to you," argued my brother.

"I disagree. You are here by divine appointment. We can work through whatever problems. Just don't give up," I pleaded.

"You don't understand, Doug. When I get up in the morning, I have to force myself to go to work. I stand in the shower and tell myself that in eternity, it will all be worthwhile. The only question is whether you will retake the pastoral position," he explained.

"Okay, I will take it back but I think it's a big mistake. I am concerned that this could divide the church. People love you and enjoy your style of leadership more than mine. God said they needed a 'new pastor' not a refurbished one," I argued.

It seemed to me that the church had gone through a major metamorphosis from being a battleship pastored by me to a pleasure ship pastored by my brother. Transitions from one pastor to another are always a dangerous time for the local church as many of the people in the pew get restless and leave.

I extracted a promise that my brother would not leave the church and go down the street and join another local church. He promised me that he would not do that.

Guess what? He did the very thing that he said that he would not do.

"You lied. You told me that you would not go down the street and join another local church," I almost shouted at him.

"I don't remember saying that but if you say that I did then I am sure that I did. You have a memory like an elephant and I would believe you over myself," apologized my brother.

His primary concern was getting his family into a safe place where they could be loved and taught. Many people were quick to tell me that they had seen my brother in church. I told them to tell my brother to repent.

This broken relationship with my brother was compounded when my brother moved 200 miles away to Chinook, Montana to pastor the local Assembly of God church. I had already been working in Chinook for over six months helping people who had left the local Assembly of God to establish an independent New Testament Church.

Six months earlier when I went to Chinook to meet with the folks, I had been told that they did not want to be a church. At the first meeting, I felt the Lord tell me to challenge the folks. "It's not a matter of whether or not you are a church but what kind will you be and how long will you last," I told the folks at the first meeting.

Later when my brother moved to Chinook, I explained to my Chinook friends that even though my brother and I had unresolved issues, he was an excellent shepherd.

"If your only issue is with your ex-pastor, you should go back to the local AG church. If you stay with me, I will spoil you with the truth of a New Testament Church," I claimed.

"It's too late. We are already spoiled. We believe you about your brother but we want something more. Something different," they chorused.

I am not sure how long it was before my brother and I were reconciled. I know that I kept confronting him until he wrote me a nasty confrontational letter.

I had way too many opinions about everything.

I read it, rejoiced and immediately called him on the phone. He started to apologize for the letter but I cut him off. I told him that he was finally getting honest and we could deal with the broken relationship.

God was so good in lovingly restoring this broken relationship. I continued to minister to the local New Testament Church in Chinook but stayed in the home of my brother. Subsequently, I preached in his church (and the two other churches that he has pastored since).

God gave me back my best friend through a process of time and confrontation. It took me many years before I could see how badly I handled the transition in our local church. I had way too many opinions (ex. battleship vs. pleasure-ship, etc.) about everything. This appears to be typical of those who father churches and don't know how to let go.

In the fall of 1987, God led me to join forces with four other men and start a regional fellowship for independent charismatic churches. We intended our fellowship to be a prototype of the covenant relationship between New Testament believers, leaders and churches.

After ten years of meetings, conferences and camps, I was asked to step down as one of the leaders. My fellow leaders stated that they perceived I was dry (a fact that I had even admitted in writing). However, the proposed solution was a total overkill. There was no moral failure or character flaw. Hindsight is 20/20 and shows that it was nothing more than believing the wrong thing and prescribing the wrong treatment.

The Christian walk is not a straight line on the mountaintops but an up and down trek. Well known Christian writer and Pastor Rick Warren says the Christian walk is more like two railroad tracks – one track is blessing and the other is suffering.

My nature is not to go silently into the night, so I vocally protested both the diagnosis and the prescribed treatment. I knew that withdrawing from leadership team would be the death of our relationship. Without function, I knew there would be no relationship.

These were my best friends in ministry and I was willing to fight through any misunderstanding. I was not willing to fade away and disappear. To be my friend meant "until death do us part."

"Why does it hurt me so much when people leave the church," I asked my reconciled brother (and best friend).

"You hurt more than me and most others because you love more than we do. When somebody leaves my church, I just tell them not to let the door hit them on the way out," confided my brother.

"What do you think I should do?"

"I think you need to shake the dust off your shoes and move on. But I know you and I know you won't do it. You will hang on until Jesus comes back."

My brother was right. Nothing I could say or do worked. The master communicator could not speak clear enough to do away with the disagreement or bring reconciliation. After a year of praying and pushing, I finally surrendered to the inevitable and resigned.

I learned that every crucifixion is unfair, unjust and undeserved.

With resignation came the largest vacuum that I had ever experienced in my heart. I literally hurt every day for a year. I felt helpless and hopeless. My brother and other well-meaning friends said, "Move on, get over it." I resisted their advice. It seemed that we were giving the devil the victory and saying our God could not reconcile brothers who said they loved God and one another.

Unlike the circumstance with my brother there has been no reconciliation even though I am still hoping and praying for it. God used this circumstance to teach me much about embracing a crucifixion. I learned that every crucifixion is unfair, unjust and undeserved.

I had to give up my right to be understood. God is the ultimate author of every crucifixion. He is never surprised by what we go through since He said that He would direct our steps and never leave us nor forsake us. A crucifixion properly embraced will ultimately make you more than you were. But improperly embraced, a crucifixion leaves you less than you were.

It is really about choice. A crucifixion will spiritually destroy you or cause you to grow in Christ beyond all previous boundaries. The crucifixion is all about death: death to self in the garden; death to sin on the cross; and death to Satan in the resurrection.

Jesus is our high priest and our example. As He is so are we in this present world. Jesus died in the garden when He said to His Father, "Not my will but Thy will be done." Isaiah 53 says that Jesus was "stricken, smitten by God" and that "it pleased the Lord to bruise Him." God made Jesus' soul an offering for sin and saw the labor of His soul and was satisfied.

Most of us spend every ounce of energy avoiding a crucifixion when it is the one thing that God might find satisfying and necessary for our spiritual growth. When the Father looked at the sacrifice of His only begotten Son, He was satisfied.

A dead man does not care who spits on him or kicks him.

The man or woman who spends their life avoiding a crucifixion has failed to position himself or herself for blessing. God is looking for "living sacrifices." When our flesh and all that it entails (pride, stubbornness, selfishness, opinions, etc.) are burned on an altar of crucifixion, God is pleased. It is like God looks down and says, "Now I can bless you."

John the Baptist spoke for all mankind when he proclaimed, "He must increase and I must decrease." God wants to bless those who are dead to self and alive to Christ. Paul said it so well when he wrote, "I live, yet not I, but Christ in me. The life I live I now live in Christ."

Christians need to be dead to self. A dead man does not care who spits on him or kicks him. He turns the other cheek, walks the second mile and gives the shirt off his back. He is different. He is a believer who is under the authority of the Lord. He has passed from death in the spirit to life in the spirit and is now dead to the old man, enjoying the life in the spirit. He has given up his self rights for the joy of knowing, loving and serving the Lord.

Even though we all want to be the perfect Christian (dead to self and alive to Christ), we come to the reality that only Jesus is perfect. He loves us even though we are marred and flawed. His excellency is in an earthen vessel (also known as jars of clay). Too many of us have been overwhelmed by disappointments, unresolved conflicts, and broken relationships. To position ourselves (or reposition ourselves) for God's blessing, we need to scrape away the disappointments.

Satan's greatest tool is discouragement. He knows that if we are discouraged we have no power. Disappointments come to all of us. Sometimes we have wrong expectations which lead to disappointment.

Where do you get your expectations? Many get their expectations about life and looks by watching television. After all, that is what television is all about. Television means to "tell a vision." When we get our vision from television, we are concerned about superficial things like cars, houses, clothes, and everything else.

If we get our expectation or vision from the wrong place, we will have the wrong vision. Psalm 62:5 says, "I get my expectation from God." God tells us what we are to think about. If there is any virtue, think on these things.

We need to deal with imaginations and or expectations that compete for our time, money and worship. The first commandment is to have "no other gods." There is a time in the life of every believer when he needs to be encouraged.

David encouraged himself at Ziklag. He came back from the battlefield to find that he had lost his family and all his possessions to a roving band of thieves. His men talked about stoning him. When there is no Barnabas (son of encouragement) to encourage us, it is our time to be Barnabas.

Disappointment over broken relationships is the most difficult thing for me to get over. I have learned to apply the principle of "scraping away the mildew" in order to be spiritually healthy and strong.

If there is mildew or mold in our house, we need to call the priest who will examine the walls (Lev 14). Many of us get it wrong – we try to hide the mildew or mold. We don't want anybody to know that we are not perfect.

But God says, "Confess your faults one to another." In the Old Testament the Levitical priest was called to examine any house suspected of having mold or mildew. Today we need New

Today we need New Testament priests to examine us and challenge us to scrape the walls of disappointment.

Testament priests to examine us and challenge us to scrape the walls of disappointment.

It is an uncomfortable process but we need to get rid of the old leaven of leprosy (disappointment). We need to be plastered with the love of God. There is nothing better than hearing the high priest say loudly and clearly, "YOU ARE CLEAN."

Many believers have neglected to encourage themselves in the Lord when they are overwhelmed with disappointment. They come to a personal Ziklag (i.e. place of deep personal loss) and allow disappointment to turn to bitterness and depression.

Disappointment always challenges us to re-connect to our source. To find God in the midst of personal disappointment is a challenge but we have a word from God that He will never leave us or forsake us.

As an optimistic Biblicist, I am determined to scrape away every disappointment. I refuse to give place to the enemy of my soul, the robber of my joy who comes daily to speak lies and point fingers of accusation.

We need to position ourselves for blessing by dying to self so that we can really live for Christ.

5

Don't Run From the Fire

Position for Blessing - Stay in the Fire

MANY OF US DO EVERYTHING within our power to avoid pain, conflict and crucifixion. We stop as soon as we have any problem or pressure. President Truman said, "If you can't stand the heat, get out of the kitchen."

Many Christians believe that if something is difficult, it's not of the Lord. How many times have we said something was God's will because it was quick and easy? Somehow we have twisted our theology into a place that says if it is hard, it must not be God.

Tell that to Moses when he was trying to lead the people to the Promised Land or to Joshua who crossed over to the Promised Land to face the giants. Tell it to Joseph who had a dream and then got sold into slavery, falsely accused of rape, thrown into jail and forgotten. Tell it to Jesus who sweated blood in the garden, was crowned with thorns and nailed to a cross.

I am an entrepreneur that likes to start businesses, buy buildings, build churches and develop ministries. I usually convince myself and my wife that it will be quick, easy and cheap. After starting dozens of businesses, churches and major ventures, I have found that my three-pronged mantra is a form of self-deception.

Even though I tell myself that it will be quick, easy and cheap, it invariably turns out to be slow, hard and expensive. It always takes longer, costs more and is never easy. It has become a bit of a joke between my wife and me.

God knows that if He let me know the real cost, I would not do it. He allows me to be deceived because He wants me to do it. God will give us the wisdom, strength and grace to overcome whatever difficulties, challenges and obstacles come our way as we move forward in faith.

Even though I tell myself that it will be quick, easy and cheap, it invariably turns out to be slow, hard and expensive.

God uses fire from Heaven to remove obstacles from our life (2 Chron 7:1-3). Right after Solomon stopped praying, God sent fire to consume the burnt offering. Then the glory filled the house. This is the way it is for many of us as we position ourselves for blessing. We want the glory without the gory. Such is not to be. As old athletes are fond of saying, "No pain, no gain."

One of the greatest fires that I ever had to go through happened in 2010 when I asked Jim Jones to return our property to us. I thought that as soon as we had the property everything would be all right but such thinking was simply another case of self-deception. My optimistic personality is unwilling to believe the worst.

I am persuaded that God loves me. If a door closes it's because God has a bigger and better door waiting to be opened. I have prayed that God give the blessing to others as I am confident of His love and commitment to me and the blessing will come as I stand fast in His love.

I have learned to pray a simple prayer, "Lord, protect me from me." By obsessing, fearing, doubting, and second-guessing, we can undo a faith decision or action. Double-mindedness is a disease common to man.

The resulting instability that comes with having two minds at the same time is common to both Christians and unbelievers. We need to think on the good things, cast down empty imaginations and bring into captivity every thought, feeling and fear. Yes, Lord, please protect Doug from Doug.

I must have failed to pray that prayer when we got back our first property in 2010 as all my vision kicked into overdrive. I want to be more than a survivor. I want to be a "thrivor." Survivors hoard their resources for a rainy day so that they can endure whatever happens.

"Lord, protect me from me."

"We need to put new flooring down and paint all the rooms of our apartment building," I told Cathy. That was the first decision that ultimately led to spending almost a year of our life and $154,000 in remodeling expense.

Thrivors do the opposite of survivors. They do more than play defense. They move forward on offense by building, remodeling and making their building into what they see in their vision. As a thrivor I did not want to merely play defense and hold onto my capital for the sake of survival. I wanted to invest in the future.

Out of this basic life philosophy of aggressive optimism, I made a decision to move quickly to remodel my twelve-unit apartment building. Little did I know or anticipate that I would enter into a time of excruciating pain (aka Hell on earth).

I would like to blame my failed friend who had withheld payments and mismanaged the trust that I had placed in him but such would be nothing but convenient revisionism. No, the decision to remodel and invest in the future was all me. I went boldly forward believing that the remodeling would be quick, cheap and easy.

God uses people and government to burn stuff out of us. In the Book of Zechariah, God used the governors of Judah like a fire among the wood. God used building inspectors to bring me to my knees as one after the next stopped us from proceeding.

"Where are your permits for the work that you are doing?" asked the friendly building inspector.

"We did not get any. I thought that if all the work was minimal and internal that we did not need to get any permits," I explained.

"We do let minor stuff go even though technically you are supposed to get a permit for even the small stuff. Show me what you are doing."

"We started out doing floors only but had a small plumbing problem which led us to replace the toilets and much piping. We also removed the old closets and replaced the kitchen counters."

"You need to stop right now. You have to have permits. This is not just minor stuff that we can pass over. I am shutting you down right now until you get a contractor and the proper building permits."

Thus began the nightmare of inspectors parading through our building making my life Hell on earth. Next came lead inspectors, health inspectors, plumbing, electrical, code, etc. ad nauseum. When my anger and frustration overwhelmed my faith, I walked away and let Kert, my administrator, deal with them.

I was so burned by the fire of the various inspectors that I am probably scarred for life. I know that God is in the refining business and that He baptizes in fire. I also know that everything will be tested by fire. In 2010, I was weighed in the balance and found wanting.

After forty years of walking with the Lord, you would think that I could withstand the fire produced by a few building inspectors. But, my desire for speed and predictability was overcome by delays and changing decisions based on which inspector showed up.

I was weighed in the balance and found wanting.

Nobody is immune from the fire. We are all "salted with fire" (Mk 9:48-50). God wants to burn up the garbage in our lives. He burns up the chaff with unquenchable fire (Luke 3:15-18).

I have traveled to the Philippines about twenty-five times to help establish God's Kingdom. I am always struck by the poverty and the smell of burning garbage. It reminds me of growing up in Sunburst, Montana where we had "burn barrels" for our garbage. I grew up with the smell of garbage, but in 2010 I smelled burning flesh - mine.

Fire tests our faith. "...that the trial of your faith, being more precious than of gold that perishes, though it be tried with fire..." (1 Pet 1:7). I want to learn to do what He wants and be the kind of person He has created me to be without the fire.

Fire is part of the Adamic curse. The first created beings were invited to walk in the Father's blessing by simply walking in the Word of God. Instead of walking in the Word, Adam and Eve listened to the Satan. This was the beginning of the fire and it's still burning through humanity today.

The really good news is that God is with us in the fire. Even when you do right like the three Hebrew children in Daniel you are not exempt from fire. Thank God for the fourth man in the fire. Thank God for protecting and preserving us in the midst of the fire.

When you sin you can expect fire NOW (Jude 7), but you can also expect God to pull you out of the fire (Jude 23). I am so grateful when God pulls me out of the fire. When the building inspectors signed final approval on my twelve-unit apartment building, God had pulled me out of another fire.

In the midst of the fire, we are tempted to make decisions that are flawed by our fear that the fire is permanent. God has not given us a spirit of fear but of love, power and a sound mind (2 Tim 1:7). Cathy and I decided to do our best to never make a decision based on fear. We know that fear is the opposite of faith.

The essence of Christianity is freedom. Fear brings bondage and causes us to make bad decisions. We think of the worst-case scenario before making a big decision. By embracing the possible negative result, God gives us the faith to go forward. I have even envisioned bankruptcy as God's plan to strip me of my pride and self-sufficiency.

The story is told of a man was preparing to cross the Sahara Desert on a camel. Just before beginning his journey, the owner of the camel said,

> "There is one more thing that I need to warn you about. You are going to experience some severe winds that will cause the sand to blow so thick that you cannot see.
>
> "Don't worry as the camel is experienced and will quickly lie down until the sand storm passes. You need to dismount and quickly lay face down next to the camel with the scarf wrapped around your face.
>
> "Now this is the most important thing I am going to tell you. Don't make any decisions during the sandstorm as it may last for hours or even days. You are going to be tempted to make big, life-impacting decisions during this time. Don't do it."

All of us have been in emotional, mental or spiritual sandstorms. Maybe it has come when a loved one died or we went through a divorce or other painful breakup. Maybe it happened when we lost a job or did not get an expected promotion. The turmoil and confusion of our circumstances cries out for a life-changing decision.

However, we need time to normalize and process. That is why wise counselors always tell people who have lost a loved one to maintain the status quo for a year or so before making big decisions. Don't make life-changing decisions in the midst of a firestorm or a sandstorm.

God told the prophet that he would take care of him during a famine (1 Kings 17:8-16). He even told him where to go. Our usual focus is on the prophet, as he is the big shot, the mighty man of God.

When the prophet showed up, the little widow was gathering sticks to make a fire. The prophet asked her for a glass of water. As she went to get it, the prophet asked her to also make a little meal for him. She stopped and told the prophet that she had nothing but a small amount of meal that she was preparing to cook for herself and her son before dying.

Don't make life-changing decisions in the midst of a firestorm or a sandstorm.

God's prophet was unmoved by her dilemma. The prophet said, "DO WHAT YOU FEAR." Give priority to God and the prophet of God. Put me first said the prophet. In the midst of her greatest time of need and distress, God sent a prophet to challenge her to put somebody else ahead of her needs and broken dreams. Do this and the Lord will take care of you.

Miracles come as we do what we fear. Many people think courage is the absence of fear but it is not. Courage is facing your fear. This is what the widow did. God's prescription for fear is to take truth – it will set you free; take love – it casts out fear; and take courage – it causes you to see Christ in your circumstance. In our story, God blessed both the widow and the prophet with provision to get them through their time of distress. Miracles happen when we put God first in our lives.

Jesus told his disciples to get in the boat and they would go to the other side of the Lake of Galilee. Once they were in the boat headed to the other side, Jesus fell asleep and a storm arose. The disciples could not believe that Jesus could sleep in the midst of the storm.

Fear gripped their hearts as they shook Jesus awake and said, "Master, we are about to perish" (Luke 8:22-25). Jesus woke up and rebuked the wind (and indirectly, the disciples who were full of fear). The storm immediately stopped and fear went away. Many preachers use this as an indictment of the faithless apostles.

I think it is a wonderful example of what we need to do when we are in the midst of a storm (firestorm, sandstorm or storm storm). WAKE JESUS UP.

I have woken Jesus up more than once when the storm became too much and fear was knocking at the door of my head and heart. Jesus is not really sleeping but making intercession for you and me. The problem is my sense of Jesus is so remote that it is like He is sleeping.

Miracles come as we do what we fear.

I know that He loves me and we are co-laborers together with him. Even when He rebukes me, He embraces me with His love. I want to be positioned for His blessing. The blessing will not come if I am so full of fear that I cannot see Him or hear His still, small voice.

Many years ago our special friend John Syratt came and led a worship seminar for our church. During part of the seminar, John challenged the group to write some original music that was relevant to the vision, doctrine and ministry of Open Arms.

Out of this came a beautiful and challenging song called *Don't Quit Waiting For Your Miracle.* One of the verses of the song says, "When your hope's gone out the window and the devil is chasing you... don't quit..."

God wants to do a miracle for you and me but we must resist the temptation to quit. Winston Churchill's short, famous speech said it all, "Never, never, never give up."

6

Naked and not Ashamed

Position for Blessing - Be Transparent

ADAM AND EVE HAD EVERYTHING that they could ever want. They had a relationship with God, their personal petting zoo, unlimited food and no need for clothes. The Scripture says that Adam and Eve were "naked and not ashamed" (Gen 2:25).

God created man in His image and likeness. Just like God, man had free will (aka sovereignty). Man could still be running around in the ultimate petting zoo eating fruit and naming animals but instead traded it all for a lie. God intended that man live by every word that proceeds out of His mouth.

Immediately after disobeying God's Word, Adam and Eve knew that they were naked. Rather than repent and humble themselves, they decided to play hide and seek with the voice of God.

Right after biting the forbidden fruit, I think Adam turned to Eve and said, “We are naked. Do you hear that?”

“It’s the voice of God. He’s walking in the garden. We need to hide. He is going to know what we did,” said Eve.

“Grab some leaves and hide over there behind that big bush. Maybe He won’t see us.”

Man substituted the law of conscience for the law of God. God’s plan was for man to walk in His effervescent light without the small light bulb of conscience. Conscience is a small candle in the dark while God’s Word is a floodlight.

While conscience is good, the Word of God is so much better. Adam and Eve lost the most powerful system of direction and intimacy – the simple Word of God. They traded it in for an inferior system called “the law of conscience.”

Man substituted the law of conscience for the law of God.

Obviously, we would rather be around somebody who has a conscience than somebody whose conscience is seared, defective or non-existent. Many criminals and habitual sinners have seared their conscience by repeatedly doing what is wrong. They have become hard-hearted. They don’t feel any guilt as nothing within them says, “I have done something wrong.” A person who commits adultery over and over obliterates guilt for sin.

Conscience is the little policeman inside your head blowing the whistle when you do something wrong. Adam and Eve heard that little policeman after they disobeyed God's direct command.

When God found His children, He asked them what they were doing.

"We were hiding because we were naked."

"Who told you that you were naked?"

God's question underscores a significant transition that has occurred in Adam and Eve. They went from the law of God to the law of conscience.

Our forefathers ran from transparency with God because of their sin. Their fear, shame and unresolved guilt led them to hide from God. Adam and Eve were snared by a wrong concept of God. They saw God as a policeman walking through the garden ready to bust them for their disobedience.

"I can see right through you."

Many people hide from God because they have a wrong concept of God. He is a loving Father looking for fellowship with His children.

God values transparency. People say, "I can see right through you." The implication is that it is a bad thing to have transparent motives and methods. Jesus commended Nathanael as a "man in whom there is no guile."

Nathanael is one of my heroes. I want to be a transparent man who has no guile or skeletons or fears. If we are secure in our relationship with the Lord, we will not put makeup on our old man.

We need to value what God values and hate what God hates if we are going to position ourselves for His blessing. When I came to Christ, I still loved my life of sin. I smiled when I remembered some of the "good old days." I had not set my affection on things above. I still loved this world.

In the early days of my Christian life, I used to pray fervently that God would cause me to love what He loves and to hate what He hates. I still pray that today, as it is so easy to start grasping for the temporary. The rich man forgot how temporary this life is and decided to tear down his barns and build bigger barns so that he could "eat, drink and be merry."

Man tends to value the visible and temporary more than the invisible and the eternal. Man values beauty, brains and brawn. We tend to idolize movie stars, singers, super businessmen and great athletes. We value looks, money, personality, Facebook, iPads and non-stop 24/7 communication. But is that what God values?

I used to pray fervently that God would cause me to love what He loves and to hate what He hates.

At Open Arms Church, we want people to know our primary values. Rather than make a long religious list (such as prayer, Bible, fellowship, worship, evangelism, etc.), we embraced the KISS (keep it simple Saints) principle. Our three primary values: intimacy with God; relationship with man; and prosperity spirit, soul and body.

Intimacy with God begins with being born again. Obviously, intimacy is aided by communication (aka prayer), fellowship and worship. What a joy to have an intimate relationship where we can sing, "He walks with me and talks with me and tells me I am His own." WOW!!!!! That is intimacy.

God created us to live in intimate relationship with Him and with His creation. John reminds us "our fellowship is with the Father" (1 Jn 1:3). We need both vertical intimacy with God and horizontal intimacy with man.

You can't force intimacy. Without mutual consent, intimacy becomes rape. Too many times we have suffered the invasion of our space by overly aggressive people wanting more than we were willing to give. While intimacy is the goal, all relationships must progress from acquaintance to casual to close to intimate.

What's stopping relationship with man? Are we too busy, too selfish, too proud, or too stubborn? Are we too fearful of being hurt, rejected or misunderstood? Many of us adopt defense mechanisms that stop intimacy and keep everything at a superficial level.

Some of the more common defense mechanisms utilized by the superficial include: treating everything as a joke (Mr. Yuk Yuk); always telling others that nobody is perfect (Mr. Pick Pick); questioning everything (Mr. No No); or barking at everybody that tries to walk on your lawn (Mr. Arf Arf).

One of my best friends would put me on notice that he did not want to go any further in an intimate conversation by sarcastically saying, "We all can't be perfect like you, Kelley." This is a method of rejecting intimacy by attacking the person who is pursuing intimacy.

Intimacy means speaking into the life of others while allowing them to speak into your life. Open rebuke is better than secret love. To be a Proverbs 27 Christian means you are willing to wound your friend.

An enlisted man asks the officer, "Permission to speak freely, sir?" Without the permission to speak freely, the enlisted man would be guilty of showing disrespect to an officer. When our relationship is less than intimate, we need to ask for permission to speak freely.

Many years ago I worked for an internationally known Christian leader. We were at a small retreat strategizing how we could be more effective in reaching our goal to recruit Christians to run for office from the schoolhouse to the White House.

During a meeting we were all shocked to see the leader fire the executive director of our political/Christian organization. When asked why he fired the man (and the manner in which he did it), the leader looked mystified and said, "When you (or the organization in this case) grow, you've got to get better people who are able to do what needs to be done."

"I believe everybody over us is corrupt and sometimes I wonder about us."

This Christian leader saw people differently than I did. He saw them as paper cups to use and throw away while I saw them as silver chalices. Even if a person had a chip or crack, you held on to them as they were made in the image and likeness of God.

After the experience with this leader, I became very cynical. I remember talking to a good friend who was at a comparable level of leadership as me.

"I believe everybody over us is corrupt and sometimes I wonder about us," I announced.

It took me ten years to get free of this spirit of cynicism. I still suffer recurring bouts when I watch Christian television or read Christian magazines.

It's impossible to become intimate with somebody who is always criticizing you. I would rather be around a positive heathen than a negative, critical Christian.

God says that the first commandment is to love God with our whole heart and soul and the second is to love our neighbor as ourselves.

"How can we say we love God whom we have not seen when we do not love our brother whom we have seen," asks God. Man is God's greatest creation made in His image and likeness. He is a spirit, which means we too must be a spirit being.

Man is a spirit that has a soul and lives in a body. The Bible teaches us that man is triune (spirit, soul and body) just like God is triune (Father, Son and Holy Spirit).

Over thirty years ago, Cathy and I attended Bill Gothard's *Basic Youth Conflicts Seminar* in Tacoma, Washington. Bill said, "God's will for you involves people."

"We see people and circumstances not as they are but as we are."

Open Arms also values prosperity – spirit, soul and body. Open Arms is full of people who have wasted 20 or 30 years of their lives lying, cheating, and stealing to support their addiction. Prosperity for our people is general relief, food stamps and Social Security.

I was having a short visit with a young black man one day and he told me what he valued.

"My greatest concern is what people think I am," he stated with resolution.

"Did I hear you correctly? Did you say that you think it is more important what people think you are than what you actually are?" I questioned.

"Yes. That's right. It doesn't matter what I am. It's only important what people think I am."

I was shocked to hear somebody openly embrace such a shallow value. It reminded me of the movie *Shallow Hal.* In this movie, Hal valued physical attractiveness over everything else.

Shallow Hal had a spell put on him so that his vision was impaired. He found himself attracted to a really overweight girl. Shallow Hal did not see her obesity but saw her as thin and beautiful.

In 1981, Creed Davis who was my father in the Lord, said the most profound thing, "We see people and circumstances not as they are but as we are." Perhaps it is merely an extension of the old maxim that "beauty is in the eye of the beholder."

The only way that we can see people and circumstances correctly is when we are the person that God intends us to be. We need to have an eternal and Biblical view of every situation. History does not revolve around us or our problem. History is literally "His story."

Humanism revolves around man while Christianity revolves around Christ. Christian humanists have been born again but put or keep man as the center of their viewpoint rather than Christ.

Image is what you think you are. Reputation is what others think you are. Character is what you are. All of these are important but the most important is character. Who are you? Are you a true Christ follower? Or are you a Shallow Hal? Too many of us have the Shallow Hal complex and have failed to embrace authenticity and transparency.

As an urban missionary to South Central Los Angeles, I have found that the values and language of a poor, black urban area are totally different than those I grew up with in Montana. When I first arrived in LA, I heard people saying that they were "dissed." Athletes and addicts alike were worried that they had been "dissed."

"I thought pride was a rich man's problem," I confided to my African-American friend.

"Have You Dissed the Lord Lately?

"I can't believe that people with no money, no homes, cars or family are worried about being 'dissed,'" I added.

My friend quickly explained, "That is the exact reason why they have this pride. Everything else has been stripped from them or forfeited by their lifestyle so they hold on to their pride."

Out of this whole issue came a message that I try to preach every year called "Have You Dissed the Lord Lately?" Too many people are worried about being dissed when they are the disser.

We diss the Lord when we say that we are Christ followers and then do our own thing. Christianity is held in contempt by many because of His inconsistent followers.

If Christians would let their "yes be yes and their no be no," the world would take notice. Christians should be the first hired and last fired because they are men and women of character who come early and leave late. They don't lie, cheat or steal. They are people of transparent integrity.

In Montana they like to tell North Dakota jokes (and vice versa, I am told). An editorialist wrote that while Montanans were busy telling jokes, North Dakotans were building a first-rate highway, educational and infrastructure system. North Dakotans have a reputation for hard work and integrity.

Having owned an employment agency for sixteen years, I was quick to hire anybody who was from North Dakota. I was confident that such a person was raised with right values (just like my North Dakota-born Mom). How much more should Christians be known as those with the right values?

Several years ago I heard a pastor preach on family values. It was different than what many of us usually think of as family values – pro-life (no abortion), pro-family (no homosexuality or pornography) and pro-God (no atheism).

He talked about a whole different set of values that he and his family embraced. It made me think of my own family values. I embraced love for God, honesty, loyalty, thinking, a merry heart, hospitality and generosity.

"I think that 'thinking' is great but to consider it a family value is a bit skewed," said my wife as she lobbied for kindness to be substituted for thinking.

Children do what we do, not what we say.

"Kelleys have always valued thinking. My dad used to say, 'Think,

think, think,'" I argued. "Kindness is a woman's fruit," I joked.

Values need to be transferred and assimilated if they are going to have any lasting effect. Employers transfer values to their employees through mission statements. Pastors transfer values to their church by what they emphasize through teaching, spending money, and promoting leaders. Government transfers values through enacting laws.

Parents transfer values to children by how they spend their time and money. As a father, my greatest fear was having Christ-less children. Values are more caught than taught. Children do what we do, not what we say.

Abraham is a wonderful example of a person giving God the absolute priority in his life. He loved God more than his own family, as seen in his willingness to sacrifice his only begotten son Isaac. We need to be like Abraham and seek God first.

If we love God, we will keep His commandments. One of His commandments is "let your yes be yes." The Bible says, "A man swears and changes not" (Ps 15). Honesty is not the best policy but the only policy.

We are admonished not to believe every spirit but test them (1 Jn 4:1). Too many Christians have a "flat nose," unable to smell the spirit of the person or circumstance standing before them. The inability to discern people and circumstances can be a ministry disqualification (Lev 21).

Only a fool believes everything. God wants us to be wise as serpents and harmless as doves. The book of Proverbs is a book of wisdom. You become smart by fearing the Lord but you need to know what God thinks.

In Mount Helena Christian Academy, a ministry of our Helena church, a special award was given to any student who memorized the entire book of Proverbs. My children have the words of wisdom rattling through their system from memorizing the book of Proverbs.

Several years ago, a friend asked me, "How come you aren't more discouraged by all the problems confronting you? It's like you are making light of everything," asserted my friend.

"I am not trying to minimize the problem but just taking God's medicine. The Bible says a merry heart is God's medicine," I argued.

Happiness is a choice. We have a big God who knows what is going to happen or a big Devil who is beating up on us all the time. We need a big God and small devil to fulfill our destiny.

Everybody has some underlying thought or philosophy that shapes his or her life and decision-making. It might be something that Dad, Mom or Grandpa said. It might be as simple as Ben Franklin saying, "a penny saved is a penny earned."

My life philosophy is "if you err, err on the side of generosity." It has relieved me from the fear of being a sucker. It allows me to leave money on the table in a business deal and feel good about it (akin to leaving the corner of the fields for the poor gleaners coming after the harvest).

My life philosophy is, "If you err, err on the side of generosity."

Many years ago I sold a van to one of the guys in our

church. We were both happy with the deal, as the price seemed fair to both of us. However, in my prayer time, I felt the Lord said to give back $500 of the purchase price. I argued a bit with God but found no other way than do what He said, so I took the $500 to my friend.

"What's this?" he asked.

"I was praying and felt God told me that I needed to refund a portion of the purchase price of the van," I said.

"Okay, but I thought the deal was fair."

Sometimes, God is testing our heart (and our pocketbook) to see if we really believe what we say we believe. Again, it is about positioning yourself for His blessing.

My wife and I place a high value on both generosity and on hospitality. We have hosted hundreds of people in our home for a night, a week or much longer.

A number of years ago we had so many people staying with us that all our adult children slept in our bedroom on the floor as friends took the other bedrooms. The good news is that I did not hear any whining or complaining. I have heard parents asking their three- or four-year-old if they are willing to give up their bed for company. Ridiculous!

I remember using a leadership questionnaire prepared by Dick Benjamin who founded a church planting movement out of Anchorage, Alaska. The potential leader was asked, "When was the last time you took somebody out for lunch or dinner?" He asked them if they tipped and if so how much.

Your values might be different than the Kelleys' values. You need to have the heart of the Lord and His values. We get God's values by praying, reading His Word and allowing people to speak into our lives. If we want all that God has for us, we need to become transparent and intimate followers of Jesus Christ.

Blessings are connected to our willingness to stand before the Lord “naked and not ashamed.” Too many times we embrace cultural fig leaves as we hide our heart from simply obeying the Lord. It is still a question of positioning for the blessing.

7

Put Your Money Where Your Mouth Is

Position for Blessing-Use Your Money for the Lord

ABOUT THIRTY YEARS AGO, I was sitting at a conference table with other leaders who were part of our family of churches. We were having a discussion about establishing a common fund to utilize for planting churches. Other churches that were committed to support outreaches utilized such a common fund. They called it an "Aaron's Fund" after Moses priestly brother.

"It's time to put your money where your mouth is," I argued passionately.

"You put your money where your mouth is," shouted back Ken McCoy, one of my best friends who was usually known for his quiet demeanor.

"We need to get on the pot or get off. Fly it or park it. I am committed and will put my money where my mouth is, but we all need to do it," I argued.

"There are too many unanswered questions about who will handle the money and what it will be used for," stated another opponent.

The discussion was more heat than light as I was the chief push for establishing the Aaron's Fund. In my zeal I failed to pre-sell the issue. I believed that the benefits would be so obvious that all I had prepared to hear was a loud chorus of "Amen, amen." The opposition was the only surface response of deeper issues of distrust.

Look at a man or woman's spending and you will quickly see what they value.

My controversial and adversarial nature loved the action but it was futile because I was pushing for something that was beyond the level of present commitment. We had failed to deal with the issues of mistrust and discontent. These are the issues that usually affect a person's willingness to give financially to projects and ministry.

The Bible says, "Where a man's treasure is, there will his heart be." We all spend money on what we value. Some buy fancy cars while others expensive clothes or houses. Some have the latest electrical gadgets and others have savings accounts.

Look at a man or woman's spending and you will quickly see what they value. A checkbook register is the clearest proof of what a person values. The checkbook does not lie. It speaks loud and clear about what we believe in.

When I first came to Christ, I did not have a history of giving. We were Catholics and Mom faithfully gave a dollar every Sunday and Holy Day. It never occurred to me that anybody gave more than this.

I had never heard about tithing. I found myself becoming suspicious and critical. Where was the money going? Was it all about money? I knew nothing about the joy of tithing and giving.

I soon learned that money, clothes, houses, cars and everything in between belongs to the Lord. A tithe was a mere reminder that God was El Eljon – the possessor of Heaven and Earth. I learned that worship was incomplete without putting my money where my mouth (and heart) was. Giving is as much an act of worship as singing *Amazing Grace.*

Some years ago when I was preaching in Mexico I felt the Lord tell me to prophesy over a man in the front row. I stopped preaching and came down from the stage and laid my hands on the man.

"The Lord wants to give you a million dollars so that you can give it to the church. Will you be trustworthy and obedient? Will you do what I say? If you will put me first, I will take care of you and your family," I prophesied.

Shortly after receiving this prophetic word, the man left the church. There is no word on whether he ever received a million dollars. It appeared to be a conditional promise based upon his willingness to give to the church.

In the early church, people were selling their property and giving the money to the apostles for the work of the ministry. Ananias and Sapphira had a piece of land that they decided to sell and give the proceeds to the church. After they sold the property, they decided to lie about how much they had received.

Ananias and Sapphira forgot that an all-knowing God was keeping the books. When they lied to the apostles, they were really lying to God. They paid with their lives for their dishonesty. It was not all about money but about truth in the inward part.

Tithing is a test of our commitment.

Tithing is about truth. We say that we love God and then we get paid, sell something or receive an inheritance. We say that God is first in our lives. Now it is show time. Do we really believe that God is first? If so, we don't lie, cheat or steal like Ananias and Sapphira.

We position ourselves for blessing by doing what we need to do. The tithe belongs to God. It is ten percent of what we earn or receive. It is easily calculated. With joy and gladness we have the privilege of bringing our offering to the Lord. It is our time to put our money where our mouth is.

Tithing is a test of our commitment. God already has the silver, the gold and the cattle on a thousand hills. He is not requiring a tithe because He is broke or desperate. We are desperate for His blessing and need to do whatever He says if we want the blessing.

I have repeatedly shared the principle of tithing with the folks who attend Open Arms. I believe so strongly that I have given them a money back guarantee.

I told the folks, "If you will tithe faithfully for six months, I will make a special agreement with you. If at the end of six months you do not see an increase in the blessing of the Lord, I will refund 100% of whatever money you tithed to the church." Even a "money back guarantee" did not result in any measureable increase in tithing.

At Open Arms folks who want to give oftentimes ask for change. Maybe they want to give a dollar and they only have a fiver. Our ushers are instructed to make change for whoever needs it. We have had people get change for a one dollar bill so they can give a quarter.

"If you are not experiencing the blessing of the Lord in your life, maybe you have robbed God," I explain.

"God does not need your money. He wants your heart. You are not the source for either God or Open Arms. It's all about you putting God first in your life," I plead with them.

Some will say, "How have we robbed God?" The Bible says in Malachi that this very question was asked and answered. God said that they had robbed Him in not giving their tithes and offerings.

God is no respecter of persons. He does not have one rule for Malachi and another for the Open Armites. You are nothing more than a thief if you don't pay your tithe and give your offering.

In 1976, I began teaching on financial freedom. Over the years the teaching grew into a 30-page syllabus full of scriptural do's and don'ts concerning tithes, offerings, money, credit cards, budgets, installment buying, work and prosperity. It's often willful sin on the part of Christians that keeps them poor.

The Bible says "poverty and shame is for those who refuse instruction." I have a church full of people who have refused instruction. It is so heartwarming when somebody breaks out and begins to practice the principle of tithing. We watch God's blessings begin to flow towards them in the form of jobs, ministry and money.

Esau's cry should be the cry of every born again believer, "Is there not a blessing for me?" Esau's father extended his hand and blessed Esau. Our Heavenly Father wants to extend His hand to bless you and me.

Jesus told His disciples that "the poor will be with you always." He did not say that you and I have to be poor. Jesus knew that not everybody would believe Him and position themselves for blessing. This is not an endorsement of the "name it, claim it" or "blab it, grab it" doctrine.

Prosperity is having all your needs met with a little left over.

Money and possessions are just one measuring stick used to measure prosperity. What about physical health? Spiritual health? Relational health? If you do not have your physical health, you have nothing. If you do not have spiritual health, it profits you nothing. And, if your life is full of empty, superficial and broken relationships, you have nothing.

The Bible clearly shows that man is triune – spirit, soul and body. God wants to bring prosperity to every area of our lives. Prosperity is having all your needs met with a little left over.

For a drug addict, prosperity is life without drugs. For a homeless person, it's a roof over his head and a hot meal.

Prosperity is very subjective. One of the problems with those who spend their lives working and acquiring is they never know when enough is enough. Do I have enough to retire? Is my IRA large enough? The materialistic acquirer never knows when to say, "This is enough."

Our forefathers in the faith used to live in Egypt - the land of not enough. Those who are not born again or have refused to leave the comfort and security of Egypt will always be living with not enough - money, security, love, friends, houses and other possessions.

They clothe their fear of losing their possessions with insurance. They have health, disability, car, house, business, umbrella, life, dental, nursing home, accidental death and any other type of insurance that they can think of to protect themselves and protect their "not enough" life.

God tells us, "The Kingdom is not meat and drink but righteousness, peace and joy." Those who live in the land of not enough need to be born again and come out of Egypt. The old song says, "Tis so sweet to trust in Jesus."

Many people want peace and joy and do everything they can to acquire it. However, true peace and joy cannot be purchased like a shirt or skirt. It comes through the righteousness of Jesus. Many of those dwelling in the land of not enough get stuck living with their pride in the land of Egypt. All they need to do is humble themselves and invite Jesus to come and be Lord and Savior of their lives.

Those who are born again come out of Egypt into the wilderness of "just enough." In the wilderness God protects them and feeds them with manna and meat as they journey towards the Promised Land.

One of the things that is so common with mankind is the need to be comfortable in their surroundings. Many became comfortable in the land of not enough and wanted to go back there when they encountered some challenges in the wilderness.

In the land of "just enough" those same people settle for less than God's blessing. They are happy pitching a tent, eating manna and worshiping a golden calf. They are afraid of the giants in the Promised Land.

It's not God's will that His people live in the wilderness vacillating between fear and contentment. God wants His children to march into the Promised Land. The spies reported that the Promised Land was a land flowing with milk and honey.

The majority report annunciated the "grasshopper doctrine" as they fearfully stated, "We were like grasshoppers in our eyes."

Grasshopper Christians spend their lives living in the land of just enough refusing to take risks. They would rather hop from church to church, throwing in a few dollars, doing a little charity work and singing a few songs while they wait for the Lord to rescue them.

Grasshopper Christians spend their lives living in the land of just enough, refusing to take risks.

The brave-hearts of Christianity choose to go to the Promised Land where there is "more than enough." The milk and honey flow for those who cross over to fight the giants and clear the land that God has given them to possess.

Milk represents our needs. God says I will meet

your need in the Promised Land. He has given us all things that pertain to life and godliness. Honey represents God's blessing of more than enough. It represents our desires. God wants to prosper us but we need to follow Him wherever He leads.

Honey might be a job promotion or your own business. It might be a three-bedroom, two-bath home. It might be a spouse and family. God wants to give you more than bare bones.

Many Christians live beneath their privilege in the land of more than enough because they have been snared with habits of survival living in the wilderness. After we take the people out of Egypt, we need to get Egypt out of the people. At Open Arms we say, "We got the believer out of the ghetto; now we need to get the ghetto out of the believer."

God wants His children to repudiate self-sufficiency and embrace His sufficiency. Many "Ghettoites" have substituted lying for truth telling, collecting recyclables or panhandling for a job. They develop methods of manipulation and self-sufficiency in lieu of trusting the Lord.

The only reality for most of them is what they see with their natural eyes. The invisible God and His unlimited resources are difficult to access.

Teaching people to be God-dependent rather than self-dependent (or government-dependent) is a hard sell. Most of our people understand government entitlement programs. They know the magic language that will allow them to receive health, food or housing entitlements.

One of the small, obnoxious habits that we have tried to break our people of is their addiction to hoarding. When we have a potluck at church, many of our people want two plates – one for now and one for later.

They don't think about those coming after them. We call this habit "greedy grabbing." We do everything we can to thwart the "greedy grabbers" from wrapping tin foil around a second plate and stashing it for later.

Sometimes it seems easier to just turn your head and ignore the obvious. However, God has called us to speak into the lives of people so that they can position themselves for blessing. They need to learn that God has so much more for them in the land of "more than enough" if they will follow His precepts and principles.

Hoarders substitute their effort for God's never-ending blessing. In the wilderness God would not allow hoarding but spoiled the hoarded manna. He wants daily dependence on Him. We do that by trusting Him for His daily bread.

Many years ago, when I was contemplating the will of God concerning running for political office, God spoke to my heart, "Occupy until He comes."

Hoarders substitute their effort for God's never-ending blessing.

A prophetic admonition from Jeremiah gave clarity to what it means to occupy. Jeremiah challenged the Israelites during their time in Babylon to take wives, have children, build houses, plant gardens and seek the peace of the city. Everybody wants the first four – the essence of the American dream.

However, seeking the peace of the city is a bit of a challenge. Do we need to do more than pray? Can we just hide out in our "bless me clubs" (aka churches) and wait for the soon coming of the Lord or do we need to do something? False prophets have always proclaimed peace when there was no peace. Is there a price to pay for true peace? If so, what is it and who is going to pay it?

Many Christians have withdrawn from this world, claiming that it belongs to the devil. This is one of the devil's big lies. When Jesus conquered death, the devil lost whatever legal claim he had to planet earth.

When the righteous are in authority, people rejoice but when the ungodly are in authority, people mourn. The Bible says righteousness exalts a nation. We need men and women willing to lose their lives (and their privacy, comfort and money) so that they can be the salt for our schools, neighborhoods, cities, states and nation.

This chapter has been about "putting your money where your mouth is." It's easy to be an armchair quarterback telling others what they should do, but it's difficult to be the one who decides. Every Christian should give money and time to political candidates.

Many people dream of winning the lottery but they never buy a ticket. John Ortberg is one of my favorite authors. His books are always humorously written to challenge the way we think. He does not write from a place of superiority but a place where the ground is level.

To position ourselves for God's continuous blessing, we need to give God total priority in our lives.

Ortberg wrote an excellent book called *If You Want To Walk On Water, You've Got to Get Out of the Boat.* God is looking for risk-takers willing to lose their lives so that the Kingdom of God can go forward.

Man measures himself and his peers by many different measuring sticks. One of the most common measuring tools is money. If you have it, you must be smart, hardworking, successful or a crook.

At Open Arms we have many folks who have successfully operated their own businesses. Their drug business generated two hundred thousand or more dollars a year. Their illegal success spoils them for the mundane life of minimum wages. God says it's better to be a doorman in the house of the Lord, than to live in the tents of the wicked. (Ps 84:10)

The cost to come to Christ has been paid in full by the sacrifice of Jesus Christ. While the gift of salvation is free, we must make choices if we desire to be blessed. The biggest choice is to give over control of our lives to the Lordship of Jesus. Being a doorman at the house of God or a drug dealer on the streets of Los Angeles is a choice.

To position ourselves for God's continuous blessing, we need to give God total priority in our lives. The prophet Haggai joined the exiles who had returned to their homeland to rebuild the temple in Jerusalem. Construction had ceased because they had experienced opposition. These believers suffered from disinterest, discouragement and dissatisfaction.

Their purpose for returning to Jerusalem was to rebuild, but the believers became more concerned about building their own houses. They were discouraged when they compared the present to the past. Looking back and desiring the good old days is a human problem.

Into this quagmire walks the prophet Haggai. He speaks emphatically while pointing the finger at the perverted priorities of God's people. Haggai shouts for all believers everywhere, "CONSIDER YOUR WAYS."

He reminds God's people that their priority is the house of God. We live for Him. He tells us to be strong and work. Then the prophet turns and gives some practical advice which is good for us today.

The prophet says DON'T TOUCH ANY DEAD BODIES (Hag 2:13-14). He establishes the simple principle of defilement. The New Testament says evil company corrupts good morals and if your hand (or friend) causes you to sin, cut it off.

"I can tell you the two most important things to help you stay clean and sober," I announced to the House of Hope.

Everything was very quiet until one eager listener hollered out, "What's the secret?"

"It's your family and friends. They don't give a damn about your sobriety. They are using and they want you to smoke along with them," I explained.

"But, my family is not like that," responded one listener.

"That's great. The Bible says evil company corrupts good morals. You walk with a fool, you become a fool. You pick your friends, you pick your destiny," I warned them.

When you make contact with dead bodies, they impart their opinions, values, habits and addictions.

Recidivism is like the problem of

people touching dead bodies. Jesus told a man who was reluctant to quickly follow him to let the dead bury the dead.

Dead bodies are those who do not know the Lord or walk in His ways. They can be friends, spouses, parents or children. When you make contact with dead bodies, they impart their opinions, values, habits and addictions. If you walk with a fool, you become a fool but if you walk with wise men, you become a wise man.

Haggai also challenges God's people to GET THE SEED OUT OF THE BARN (Hag 2:19). The seed does no good warehoused in the barn. Seed is meant to be planted in the field where it will reproduce. The prophet says that God wants to bless you. Again, you will not be blessed if you touch dead bodies or leave your seed in the barn.

Money is what is exchanged for work. Money always follows service. Too many people want to be paid just to show up. God challenges us to work hard. He says, "Whatever you do, do heartily unto the Lord."

Too many Christians are looking for lions in the street so that they can justify doing nothing.

All mankind breaks into two groups – the blessed and the unblessed. The "unblessed" include lazy people (Prov 21:25-26), sleepers (Prov 6:10-11), pleasure seekers (Prov 2:17), and drunkards and gluttons (Prov 23:21). One of my favorites is the clever unblessed man who excuses himself from work because "there is a lion in the street" (Prov 22:13).

Too many Christians are looking for lions in the street so that they can justify doing nothing. Some of the lions in the street include lack of education, a criminal record, a lack of experience and on and on. The Master rebukes “Mr. One Talent” for burying his talent instead of investing it. The Master says, “You should have put my money to interest.”

If you want to be blessed, you need to be a doer of the Word of God (Rom 14:22). God says that doers are happy. He says that in all work there is profit (Prov 14:23) and that work is honorable (Ps 111:3). It’s been said, "If you want to get something done, give it to a busy person.”

When I first started working as an attorney, I found it difficult to resurrect the necessary enthusiasm and brain cells to do the work unless I had a stack of work. So, I would wait until I had a stack and then I would attack it with every ounce of intellectual energy that I had. I would go in early, stay late and do whatever it took to accomplish the purpose.

Many people are depressed because they have no work that is meaningful. During the sixteen years that we owned a personnel business, we learned that money was only one of the many factors that caused people to get out of bed and go to work. Many people crave praise more than money. They want somebody to notice them and their accomplishment. We have learned to praise publicly and correct privately.

The unemployed need to go to a food bank, school, church or other place and volunteer. Get out of bed and go to work as a volunteer or as one searching for a full time job. Too many people quit their existing jobs because they are unhappy. They need to hold on and work even harder until they find a better job.

Oftentimes, we are the problem, not the job or the boss. We have a bad attitude and God wants to deal with that before He takes us to another place.

Again, you position yourself for the blessing when you have a right attitude and work hard. God says it so well when He says "faith without works is dead." James challenges the super spiritual (and possibly lazy) that he will show them his faith by his work.

What about you? What does your work say about you? Maybe God is telling you to "put your money where your mouth is."

8

"Do Whatever He Says"

Position for Blessing - Obey Him

MANY YEARS AGO I READ a small book by Loren Cunningham, the founder of Youth With a Mission (YWAM), called *Hearing the Voice of God.* It was such a wonderful challenge to me that I bought a case of the books and gave them to everybody I knew. My greatest commitment is to do only what He says.

Jesus did His first miracle at the wedding feast in Cana as a result of a believing mom exhorting the servants to "do whatever He says." It is still the best advice ever given by a mom.

Too many times we are willing to do anything and everything except what "He says." We have many excuses for not doing what He says. The biggest problem is a hearing problem. Our ears are so full of the noise of this world that we can't sort out the still, small voice of God.

The world screams at every problem and situation while the Lord whispers. God is not interested in raising His voice or enlightening the heathen. He told his disciples that, "I speak these things in parables so that you will see and understand while the world will not."

The first time (and only time) that I ever spoke in a Lutheran church, my message was on hearing the voice of God. I told the story of little Samuel not recognizing the voice of God when God called his name. Samuel mistakenly ran to Eli to see what he wanted until Eli discerned that it was God desiring to speak to the young boy. Eli instructed Samuel to remain quiet and simply tell the Lord that he was ready to listen. The Bible says that Samuel's problem was that he did not have a relationship with the Lord.

"To know Him, to know Him is the cry of my heart...To hear what He's saying brings life to my bones."

Most people are just like Samuel – they cannot hear God's voice because they have no relationship. The Bible says that there are many voices in the world. How do we discern the voice of God in the midst of the clamor and clanging of so many voices?

We are blessed when we hear the voice of God and do what He says. Every voice needs to be traced to its place of origin. Even the voice of the donkey speaking to Balaam had an origin. God was using the vocal cords of the donkey to speak a message to the rebellious, headstrong prophet who was going in the wrong direction.

There are three different voices – God, man or the devil. When Gideon heard a voice telling him to tear down the devil's altar, he was unsure of who was speaking to him so he asked for confirmation. He asked the Lord to wet the fleece while making everything around it dry.

After God did that, Gideon wanted more proof so he asked God to reverse the process by making the ground wet and the fleece dry. God was both gracious and longsuffering in confirming His word to Gideon. Out of this story comes the principle of "fleecing." Rather than simply believe God, many Christians "fleece God".

"Fleecing" is not an extension of faith but of fear. You are telling God that you are not sure that He is speaking and you want additional evidence. It is not wrong to ask the Lord to confirm something in the mouth of two or three witnesses. The Bible tells us that we should expect confirmation when the Lord is directing us. The song *To Know Him* says, "To know Him, to know Him is the cry of my heart...To hear what He's saying brings life to my bones."

If our dried-up bones are going to live, they need to hear what He is saying. He is the marrow in our spiritual bones. He is the one giving direction to our feet. Christianity is not about me but it is all about Him.

About twenty years ago, the Lord impressed me to share Mathew 4:4 which says, "Man shall not live by bread alone but by every word that proceeds out of the mouth of God." It was not a one-time message but to be read and commented on every time I spoke for an entire year. God wanted to impress upon me that my primary job was to hear His voice.

Everything else is secondary to the sound of His voice. Mary understood this as she sat with open ears at the feet of Jesus while her sister Martha was busy preparing a meal.

The present church has far more Marthas than Marys. Mary sits at the feet of Jesus because there is only one thing that is necessary. Yet we need to be like Martha, willing to get off our spiritual butts and do the work of the ministry.

God has called us to first hear what He is saying and then act on it. An invisible God speaks to His disciples every day in the midst of the noise and circumstances of this world. The hardest time for a believer is when he is uncertain of what God is saying. This is a time of waiting and standing still to see the salvation of the Lord. He has promised a blessing to those who wait on the Lord.

Real friends don't tell you what you want to hear but what you need to hear.

How do we know if something is really a word from God and not self or the devil? The first way is to discern if it is scriptural, as God will never, never contradict His Word.

When my soul gets wrapped around an issue, I lose my ability to discern. Objectivity has been thrown out the window and I am left to emotion and intellect to figure it out. At times like this, I turn to my closest friends and confess that I need their discernment, as I have gotten too close to hear clearly. Real friends don't tell you what you want to hear but what you need to hear. Most of us hate it when we lose control.

Well, that is what happens when our soul gets wrapped around buying a red convertible BMW or something else.

We don't want to hear about the payments, the cost for repairs or the hundred other thoughts of the naysayers. We just want somebody to say "buy it" so that we can wrap our teeth around our bone and hold on no matter what. The world says, "You only live once."

As a prolific visionary, I eat vision every day. This does not mean that every vision is from the Lord. Some visions come out of my nature to look for greener pastures. I need to test every word that I think that I am receiving from His Spirit. Is it consistent with everything God is speaking at this time? Does it bear witness with what the Spirit has been saying to me?

God is not silent. Every decision that has been good in my life has its origin in the Lord. His still, small voice that spoke to the prophet in the cave is the voice that I need to hear. Elijah ran from Jezebel who said she was going to kill him because Elijah had killed her false prophets.

He ran into the wilderness and said, "It's enough!" Elijah was out of faith even though God had used him in such a powerful way. However, God had a better plan and sent the birds to feed and strengthen him so that he could run to his divine appointment in a cave.

In the cave Elijah told God that everybody was gone and that he was the only one left. Like many of us, Elijah was moving on human emotion and spiritual deception. God sent the wind, the earthquake and the storm but God was in none of these spectacular events. Instead, God was in the still, small voice.

It was this voice that spoke into the life of Elijah. He rebuked Elijah for his deception and told him that He had 7,000 who had not bowed their knee to Baal. Then God gave Elijah a specific assignment to go and anoint Elisha.

Obviously, the word of God was just what Elijah needed to restart his faith and resurrect his purpose.

If you are beat down by life, get into your cave (aka prayer closet) and wait for the still, small voice of God. It's a wonderful thing to hear the whisper of the Lord. Like little Samuel we need to say, "Speak Lord, your servant hears."

God's voice seldom comes to us in an audible manner unless He chooses to speak through another person. God chooses the instrument through whom He will speak. One day when I was in law school, I was wrestling with a particular decision and could not seem to find the mind of Christ when a disbelieving fellow student spoke up. Instantly my spirit knew that God was speaking through the mouth of this modern day jackass and all I needed to do was hear and obey.

God first spoke to me in September, 1970 through the hearing of His Word. When I heard First Corinthians 10:13, I sobered up and was filled with faith. Faith comes by hearing the Word of God and that night I heard the Word. God said He would not allow me to be tempted beyond my ability. He had a plan that He called a way of escape.

Even though I was a macho man who did not want any crutches, I desperately needed healing and wholeness for the emptiness that filled me on the inside. The greatest night of my life was the night I humbled myself and received the free gift of salvation. As the old song says, "Oh, the joy that floods my soul."

At the time I received Christ, I had a summer job working as a laborer for a plumbing firm before starting law school. The week immediately following my salvation, I heard the word, "Don't eat," which led to a week of fasting. For the first week of my spiritual life, I feasted on the words in the big, black borrowed Bible. I found the passage where

Jesus said, "I have food that you know not of. My food is to do the will of God." This verse alone sustained me for a week.

As I look back on forty years of walking and working with the Lord, I find that my life has been filled with His words of love, encouragement, correction and direction. John Wesley said, "The world has never seen what can be accomplished by one man totally sold out for Christ. By God's grace, I will be that man."

Revelation 19:10 says, "Prophecy is the testimony of Jesus." His voice brings strength, stability and purpose to our lives. In the Gospel of John we are told that we are sheep and we know His voice. He calls us by name and we follow Him (Jn 10).

There are many voices in the world (1 Cor 14:10) and none without significance. But when it comes down to it, there are three voices and three choices – the voice of God, man or the devil. The voice of man comes from within and is soulish and selfish. I hear this voice constantly as it is concerned about comfort, pleasure, food, drink, friends and fun. This is the "me-oriented" voice.

But there is also the voice of the devil that comes from without and always leads us away from God. The devil's voice flatters, pampers and deceives. Oftentimes, the voice of Satan merges with the voice of man so that it can be louder and more persuasive.

Satan is quick to say "you deserve this" or "it won't hurt anything" or "nobody will know." I know this voice as it has spoken to me many times. I wish that I could tell you that I always tested the spirit and was never deceived by the deceiver but such would be untrue. When Satan joins with self, it double-teams our spirit man to do what the old flesh-man wants to do.

The voice of God comes from within our spirit or from above. His voice speaks specifically and not just generally. He leads us to maturity and holds us accountable. He reminds us of specific principles and precepts and rightly divides His Word.

"The world has never seen what can be accomplished by one man totally sold out for Christ. By God's grace, I will be that man."

God will not be defined by our religious limitations, expectations and superstitions. Satan only counterfeits something of value. His counterfeit guidance system ranges from false prophecy and ungodly counsel to Ouija boards, fortune telling and astrology.

We can expect God to confirm his Word through two or more witnesses (2 Cor 13:1). God is willing to repeat Himself because He knows that we are like little children busy playing (and sometimes praying but not listening). It's not wrong to wait on the Lord for confirmation of His Word. However, we must remember that Christianity is ultimately a faith walk. The worst thing we can do is minimize, procrastinate and disbelieve when God has spoken with clarity about something.

This small book is about positioning for God's blessing. There is no more important principle than hearing the voice of God. We say in business that a multitude of sales can overcome a pile of bills. The same is true when it comes to the voice of God. The glory of the Lord comes through hearing His word – both the Scriptures and His Holy Spirit.

When we think that we have heard God's voice, we apply the three-finger test – the finger of God, finger of self and finger of others. Is it scriptural? Does it bear witness to my spirit? Do others bear witness to it?

The voice of God is a gift of love from our God who said that He would never leave us nor forsake us. Every gift has three parts – donative intent, delivery and acceptance. The Bible says that the word did not profit them because it was not mixed with faith. He told His disciples before His ascension to Heaven that He would send a Comforter who would guide us and teach us while convicting the world of sin.

Our natural fathers want to give us good gifts. Many of them sacrifice and work hard to put us through school, help us buy a house or start a business. Our Heavenly Father has given us His voice and chosen His Word and Spirit as the delivery system. Will we accept or reject this precious gift?

When we think that we have heard God's voice, we apply the three-finger test...

Shortly after I came to Christ, I sensed that the Lord wanted me to "put my Isaac on the altar." My Isaac was not a person but a plan. I had mapped out a plan to become Governor of Montana. It was very time specific and focused on various electoral steps. However, I had not contemplated the intervention of the Lord changing everything.

God's first words saved me and took me from being a child of the devil to being a child of God. His next word was a test of my total commitment to Him. Peter said it so well when the Lord asked him and the other disciples if they too would leave Him. Where would we go, what would we do, you have the words of life was the response of Peter. He spoke for all of us with this verbal commitment.

The Lord faithfully opens and closes doors. From jobs to purchases, God has been faithful in guiding and directing. Baby Christians believe if something is painless and easy that it has to be God. I have found the opposite to be true. Narrow and hard is the way that leads to blessing. The will of God is like going through a maze (just like the people in the wilderness).

One of my most favorite people in the whole earth is a wonderful woman pastor named Margaret Van Camp who says, "God will lead you the easiest way you let Him."

Too many of us fight the Lord when He wants to lead us in marriage, our job or our purchases. We can get our soul wrapped around a particular idea and refuse to give it up. We become like the monkey that is trapped with his hand in a jar. The monkey refuses to let go of the object and withdraw his hand even when it means his freedom.

"God will lead you the easiest way you let Him."

I use the "clean blackboard" to prevent the intrusion and obstruction of self-will. I think of what I want, write it down and then intentionally wipe it off the board. What I really want is more than a house, a car, a promotion or anything else.

I want Him. I want His will, His plan, His blessing. I want what He will give me more than what I have earned through forty days of fasting. Jesus spoke for me in the Garden when He said, "Not my will, but thy will be done." To really serve Christ effectively, we need to die to self.

In 1975 I was the County Attorney in Garfield County, Montana and had a nice law practice when God spoke into my life. He said, "You are not long for that place." I was so convinced that it was the Lord speaking that I went home and sold my 24-foot yacht and vacant lot.

Subsequently, I accepted an invitation to be the Lieutenant Governor candidate with a born again state senator. Such a race seemed like foolishness, as the nomination was all but won by the incumbent attorney general. However, the Lord reminded me of the word that I was "not long for that place."

I withdrew as the county chairman for the attorney general's nomination and agreed to run. I bought a small motor home so that my pregnant wife and I could drive all over eastern Montana asking people to vote for us. We made a mad and passionate dash for the finish line but came in second. I believed that "obedience is better than sacrifice."

Green-light Christians assume that God is directing their path and that everything is go, go, go....

Christians choose to live their lives one of two ways – as a green-light or red-light Christian. Green-light Christians assume that God is directing their path and that everything is go, go, go unless God puts up a stop sign, red light or impenetrable barrier. Red-light Christians wait for God to change the circumstance before they go forward. They are overly concerned about missing the will of God.

The green-light guys (of which I am one) recite Philippians 3:15, "Therefore, let us, as many as are mature, have this mind; and, IF IN ANYTHING you think otherwise, GOD WILL REVEAL even this to you." In its context, this challenge is to press into the calling of God.

All Christians know that God says the steps (and stops) of the righteous are ordered of the Lord. But do we live like that?

What a kick it is to be a Christian and know that God is never surprised by our circumstances. He knew about that misunderstanding or demotion before it ever happened.

Tom Peters wrote a book for business people called *In Search of Excellence.* Peters set out principles found in successful companies. One of the principles he called "bias for action." Successful companies did not spend time over-thinking and over-analyzing an idea. Instead of the usual "ready, aim, fire" many successful companies simply went to "ready, fire."

We Type A personalities love to find justification for those things that affirm our impulsiveness (go Peter go). Although I did not win the political race in 1976, I continued to wait and prepare for the pending departure. God had given me a word, "You are not long for that place." It was just a question of His timing.

On February 10, 1977, I woke up in Helena, Montana and heard God say, "It's time to move." At noon I was having lunch with Greg Jackson – my best friend from law school. As we visited, he asked me what was happening in my life. I told him that I was moving. He asked me where I was moving. I told him that I didn't know. He asked me what I was going to do. Again, I told him that I didn't know.

I shared with Greg that God had spoken to me in 1975 that I was "not long for that place" and that this morning He said it was time to move. Greg was a committed believer and quickly told me that God had been stirring him to make a change. He was contemplating leaving the law firm that he was with and setting up his own practice.

We agreed to fast and pray for God's plan. Within days it became evident that God was involved in this whole move. It required faith to agree with God and risk being judged as an impulsive fool. But by telling my friend that I was moving, I mixed the word of God with faith. Taking risks is one of the key principles for positioning yourself for God's blessing.

In 1980, after several years of law practice, we had a special time in our little church plant. We invited four prophetic men to come and pray over those of us in the church and share whatever God told them. Finally, it was our turn to be presented.

The prophet spoke loudly, quickly and emphatically, "You are the shepherd. I have called you to serve me and serve my people. Don't look to the right or to the left for somebody else to do it. You are the one I have called." Each of the other three prophets brought a confirming word.

This was a difficult word for me. I had a great law partner and was the Republican candidate for state senate. This word caused me to again change directions. I was more sure that God wanted me to accept the call to pastor than become a state senator (or governor).

"Do you think that I should withdraw as a candidate for the Montana State Senate?" I asked Linnis Perry, the lead prophet.

"Hey, I shoot them, you clean them," said the prophet.

"What does that mean?"

"It means that we have done what we were supposed to do. We prayed, heard from God and spoke the word over you and the others. Now it's your turn to interpret and apply the word. Our job is done," explained Linnis.

As I was driving home from the prophetic meetings with Cathy and Pastor Gary Kroeze (an intense brother from Choteau, Montana), I asked Gary what he thought I should do about the campaign for State Senate. Without hesitation, qualification, equivocation or explanation, he spoke two words, "FORSAKE ALL."

Withdrawing from the political race was painful but necessary. I believed that the Isaac that was not killed in 1971 was now dead. God's blessing comes from doing what He says.

God blessed that decision as He faithfully built His church. Although God continued to speak, the next life-challenging word came in 1984 when the Lord spoke, "The church has become monastic and needs to go back to the marketplace."

At the time of this word, I was in the process of moving our church even further from a place of relevance. The Christian book *Living Together in A World Falling Apart* influenced me. The early Christians shared their lives in a community together with a common purse.

I had already experimented with the principle of Christian communalism by having our friends, Marv, Brenda and Yvette Woith move into our home. We pooled our money together in various envelopes and wrote on the outside of the envelope the date, amount and type of purchase. It was great in theory but this flirtation with community did not work. As we analyzed the problem, it seemed that we were obliterating the authority of the individual family.

Before we export a great Biblical theory to our congregation (or write a book about it) we need to hook it up to our own life. We tried the home school even though we had a private school and found the challenges too great for most of our people. The same was true with placement of two families under one roof. We want God's will and Word, not man's scheme and dream.

This book is about finding and receiving all that God has for you. His will is like a treasure hunt. The man who found the buried treasure went and sold everything he had to buy the field. Many of us are unwilling to sell all that we have to buy the field. The rich young ruler was unwilling.

I want to be the man who says yes to anything and everything that God calls me to do. What does it profit a man to gain the whole world and lose his own soul? We can't take it with us. In a very real sense, the Christian walk is a treasure hunt.

Many years ago I was in between pastorates (a dangerous time for visionaries) so I had nothing to do but start businesses. We know that God has pioneers who go out and start things from scratch, remodelers who remodel and maintainers who refuse to rock the boat. Different gifts and different callings determine what we are and what we do.

I want to be the man who says yes to anything and everything that God calls me to do.

Pioneers come first, blazing a trail where no man has gone before (for all the Star Trekkers out there) while the settlers come later. The settlers come to organize choirs, start Sunday Schools, men's meetings, ladies' meetings and every other type of ministry. One is not better than the other. A major problem is when those called to pioneer stop pioneering and get caught up in the process of development (choirs, VBS, etc.). This is a good time to abide in your calling.

“Pastor Doug, how long do you intend to pastor Mount Helena?” asked one of my church members (aka a thorn in the side).

“Well, I’m forty five now. I think I have another ten years in me before I go to greener pastures,” I explained, knowing that his inquiry was nothing more than an assessment to determine if he could outlast me.

“Oh, I thought you might have something else that you wanted to do,” said the talking thorn.

So I was a bit surprised a few years later when the Lord spoke through my spiritual father, “Your plans are not my plans.”

The Lord had graciously greased the slope of my departure from pastoring Mount Helena Community Church. Having been unhelpful in the earlier transition with my brother, I thought the best thing I could do was move geographically as I turned over the reigns of the church to my law partner Bryan Asay.

This is always a dangerous time for a visionary as you see possibilities, needs and opportunities everywhere you go. During this time I envisioned overseeing ten businesses and ten churches. I had a boat marina, a law practice, three restaurants, a travel agency, rental property and a personnel business. At the same time I was giving oversight (or apostolic input) into about seven churches.

It was a great vision but offered no rest as there was always a problem somewhere. I always accepted one more business, church or ministry assuming that I could manage my time better and become more efficient. I was well into my middle and late forties before I began to see that I was not superman.

I was shocked when I looked at the big "S" on my chest, as I was certain that it was a big "S" for Superman. Instead of Superman, it said STUPID. I was working hard climbing every economic, business and spiritual mountain that was in front of me. In 1994, too many bills and too little help were dragging down Cathy and me.

It was during this time that I looked for small times of rejoicing. On my birthday in 1995, I was excited to wake up and give myself a birthday present. It was the day that I was going to "fire Bob." I had had numerous clashes with one of the young lawyers who was working for us. He loved to irritate and aggravate.

He put up a large Confederate flag and then argued with me when I told him to take it down. That was just one of many issues that brought us to a need to part ways. He was intelligent and capable enough but it was not a good fit.

I was certain that it was a big "S" for Superman. Instead of Superman, it said STUPID.

By this time we had established a second law office in Lakeside, Montana where we moved after turning over the church to my law partner who was an elder.

I normally don't rejoice in firing people, but this had gone on long enough and everybody knew this day was coming. So, I woke up on the morning of my birthday for a quiet time before going to the office to give Bob the good news. Before I could even drink my first cup of coffee, I heard the still small voice of God whisper in my ear, "Don't fire Bob. Fire yourself."

"No, Lord. How can I fire myself? I own the business. My name is on the door." I protested. Quickly, the Lord ministered clarity to me that my call was in the church and ministry not the law business.

"Hey, Bob, I need to see you. Come to my office and bring Jim (his friend and fellow lawyer working for us)," I said as soon as I got to the office. Bob looked like he knew what was coming as he and Jim took seats in front of my desk.

"Don't fire Bob. Fire yourself."

"I have an offer that I want to make to you guys. I will sell you the Lakeside law office," I said as I regarded the shocked look on their faces.

"Is this a trick? Are you just trying to get rid of us?" asked Bob.

"No. I am dead serious. I know that you have been talking with my old friend, Channing Hartelius, who has a law practice in Great Falls and a residence here in Lakeside. Maybe he will put up the money to buy me out," I explained.

"But you would have to sign a covenant not to compete."

"That would be no problem. You both know that my passion is the church and the ministry. If you want to do this deal, you need to step on it right away," I told them.

After they recovered from the shock and were assured that there was no trick, we worked out the details including a covenant not to compete. I never told them that I was doing this in obedience to God, as it was not relevant to them. Within a week or so the papers were drawn up and the deal was made.

It's such a joy to have the Lord counseling, inspiring, leading and correcting as we live our lives. In October, 1996 as I was praying, God impressed on me that He was going to "take those trained in the wilderness and move them to the cities." I thought this was a good prophetic word but was not sure for whom.

At the time, I was a big man in a small pond. I was the "Jerry Falwell of Montana." I knew all the movers and shakers across the Big Sky Country. I was the cowboy from Montana known and loved by some and despised by others.

A year later I knew God was telling me that I was the one that needed to move to the city. In early 1998 I was invited to move to Burbank, California to work with Ralph Mahoney and his mission organization World MAP. We embraced this as fulfillment of the word spoken to us. We sold what we could sell, packed what we needed into a U-Haul and headed down the highway to our new destiny.

Many folks have said, "It must have been hard to move from beautiful, pollution-free Montana to the crime and grime of Los Angeles."

To the contrary, staying would have been hard. We had a word from God. In Him we live and move and have our being. We were born to serve Him and Him alone. We did not change locations. We were in Christ in Montana and we would still be in Christ in Los Angeles.

Since relocating to California, we have continued to depend upon the Lord's still, small voice to guide us into making righteous decisions. From starting a church to filing a lawsuit (and everything in between), we have needed and depended on finding the mind of Christ and being guided by the peace that passes understanding.

God brings a prophetic challenge to our lives like "move from the wilderness to the city." After the challenge comes the prophetic compliance when we embrace and act upon what has been spoken. Then comes the prophetic crisis where the word of the Lord is tested. (Ps 105:17-19) Ultimately there is a prophetic consequence where the word comes to pass (or not) as a result of our mixing it with faith (Heb 4:2).

The old nature always resists what God is saying by doubting and disputing. The resisters end up quoting Satan when they think or say "did God really say?" God is looking for a prophetic people who will hear His Word and do it regardless of the consequences.

God is not interested in excuses but in total obedience.

When God brings a prophetic challenge, He initiates it. The challenge is beyond what you can do in the natural and will lead you to places you have never gone before. God is the most creative travel agent there ever was. We see Joshua receiving a prophetic challenge from God. This was Joshua's moment to do signs and wonders and stretch his faith (Josh 3).

Without faith it's impossible to please God. Christianity is all about the just walking by faith. We are faith-walkers. We see an invisible God and serve Him in expanding His Kingdom to whosever will. God looks on our hearts. He fills us with His wisdom and courage.

God is not interested in excuses but in total obedience. We need to do whatever He says. This is where the blessing of the Lord comes upon us.

9

What are You Waiting For?

Position for Blessing - Wait on the Lord

THE WORLD SHOUTS OVER EVERY FEAR "just make a decision." Conventional wisdom says even a bad decision is better than no decision and that no decision is actually a decision. While these thoughts have a measure of truth, the real problem is our impatient nature.

We retain our child-like impatience, asking repeatedly, "Are we there yet?" We are uncomfortable waiting for something to happen. After all, we are the masters of our own fate, the captains of our own destiny. Wrong!!!

We are children of God called by Him to put to death the old man and live in newness of life. In patience we possess our souls. Many of us have a hyper-active soul-life unable and seemingly unwilling to simply sit down and shut up.

Waiting is a learned behavior that some of us have not yet mastered.

I tell my wife, “I don’t do lines.” If there is a long line at a restaurant, I drive on. Oh, I know, the food purists believe that the long line validates the restaurant. Having owned three restaurants, I loved it when we had a line and were working hard to turn tables. However, standing in line to buy something seems a colossal waste of time.

The truth is that all of us are waiting for something. Some are waiting for a job, others for a spouse and others for a geographic or educational revelation. Much of our life is waiting for something to happen or somebody to do something. We wait for money or a better job, wisdom or direction, healing or reconciliation, forgiveness or fulfillment. In a real sense we are professional waiters.

Our reaction to waiting varies from person to person. The Bible says that God is changing us from glory to glory. The “to” stage is the waiting process. It’s easy to get lost in the glory of His presence or the answer to a prayer. It’s difficult to simply wait.

The Word tells us to abide in our calling. This is another way of saying wait. Stand still and see the salvation of the Lord. They that wait upon the Lord shall renew their strength.

Some of us wait with fear. and anxiety, wringing our hands, playing out the possible scenarios over and over in our heads. Some of us are overcome with impatience and frustration and talk and talk and talk. We are full of questions and confusion. We vacillate between fatalism and passivity. Godly contentment seems to be nothing more than a delusion or deception.

It's during this time of vulnerability that many of us become "do-it-yourself Christians." The world has changed from full service gas stations to self service. We book our own travel online, use ATMs and even receive and pay our bills online.

Our obsessive/compulsive natures no longer have to wait on anything or anybody in the great information age. With a hand-held computer we can rule the world by communicating with family and friends on Twitter, Facebook or some other social communication system.

A Biblical picture of do-it-yourself Christians is seen throughout the Bible. Egypt is visible, always appealing to the senses while God appeals to the spirit. Do-it-yourself Christians are rebellious, independent, sinful, stupid, deceived, lying and childish.

Many of us become "do-it-yourself Christians.

God warns Mr. Self-Sufficiency that he will be humiliated and shamed. The impatient believer loves to quote, "I can do all things through Christ who strengthens me." He says, "I have a fast horse" (Ps 20:7).

Waiting is one of the hardest things we do. Yet it is also one of the most profitable times, as all the un-crucified flesh comes rising to the surface where it can be offered to the Lord. A bias for action is a characteristic that marks a successful company or Christian champion.

Waiting might appear to be the opposite of action but it is not. True waiting is not forced passivity but actively seeking His voice, His face, His plan. It is prayer, fasting, and counsel.

In the movie *Gandhi*, Mr. Gandhi was asked how long he had been a pacifist. Gandhi looked at the questioner and said in the strongest voice he could muster, "I have never been a pacifist in my life." He saw peaceful resistance as the opposite of passivity. Passive people sit and wait for somebody else to do something but such is not true of those who are waiting on the Lord.

Phillip Brooks, a well-known New England preacher, was known for his quiet, scholarly, patient demeanor. One day he appeared out of character, pacing back and forth in an agitated manner. His wife noticed his unusual behavior.

"What's the trouble, honey? It's not like you to be pacing and restless," she noted.

"The trouble is that I am in a hurry, but God isn't," replied Brooks.

This is the problem for many of us. We are in a hurry but it appears that God isn't. God's concept of time is so different than ours. He is the Alpha and Omega, the Beginning and the End. He is infinite and timeless. With God, a day is like a 1,000 years.

Waiting on the Lord is one of the greatest principles to experiencing His blessing. I have pressed God in prayer thousands of times to do something NOW. Give me money NOW. Help me lose weight right NOW. Send me leaders NOW. I am ashamed to admit it, but much of my forty years of prayer life has been one small demand after the next. My mind says, "I need, I need, I need it NOW."

Why does God not act more quickly to save me? There is a story in 2 Kings 19 where God's people were under attack from their enemy. Because the enemy had surrounded them and had cut off provision for food and commerce, they were suffering.

Sennacherib, the leader of the Assyrians, tried to deceive God's people into surrendering without a fight (sounds like the devil to me). He pumped the people full of his fear-filled message. Instead of using a surprise attack or a direct assault, Sennacherib chose to put God's people under a siege. His plan was to wear them down through cutting off their communication, food and other resources.

Values change when you are under siege. Things that would be totally repulsive become acceptable and justifiable because your mind cannot find an alternative. God's people bought a donkey's head and dove droppings to eat (2 Kings 6:25). They even ate their own children. Part of the enemy's strategy during a time like this is to get people to turn on one another. The king blamed Elisha for the suffering and concluded WHY SHOULD I WAIT ANY LONGER?

God spanks His children as an act of love and direction.

God's ultimate purpose is not the comfort of the saints. He is the God of all comfort and Father of mercy; however, His primary purpose is to change man into His image. He created man to have dominion and to have fellowship with Him.

Self-sufficiency stands in the way of His primary purpose. His image is not seen in the self-made man. Limited, superficial fellowship awaits those who refuse to die to self.

God spanks His children as an act of love and direction. He is not content to let us do our own thing, even though He has given us that power and freedom. His spanking is evidence of His love and our legitimacy. He trains us and makes us profitable servants through whatever discipline He places in our lives (Heb 12.)

No spanking is fun at the time. We need to take God's spankings as validation of our son-ship and preparation for the future. The trouble for too many of us is that we are in a hurry and God is not. He has the long view of every situation and circumstance where we are simply trying to muddle our way through without losing our sanctity, sanity or sainthood.

I admire people who can do things that I want to do but can't do because I lack the gifting, know-how or character. I admire the man or woman who can wait silently for the Lord (Ps 62). Oftentimes, we need to battle through the confusion and the questions as we are in the middle of the sandstorm and tempted to make a decision based on our pain and incomplete information.

I have met a few silent souls waiting on the Lord. My soul tends to be a bit noisy asking questions, talking too much and saying nothing.

In 2 Kings 5 we read about a man named Naaman who came to the prophet Elisha to be healed of leprosy. Elisha has his servant Gehazi tell him to go dunk himself in the Jordan seven times. Naaman overcomes his initial anger and reluctance and does what he is told.

My soul tends to be a bit noisy...

Of course, God heals Naaman of his leprosy. Naaman is so grateful that he comes back to Elisha with gifts to thank him for this great healing. However, Elisha refuses the reward so that God will get all the credit.

Gehazi must have been the great-grandfather of Judas Iscariot. "We had a chance to make a killing from this rich Samaritan," thought Gehazi, as he secretly ran after Naaman and told a lie in order to get a small amount of money and two suits. When Gehazi returned from his trip to the dark side of disobedience, Elisha asked where he had gone.

Gehazi lied to Elisha. Although Elisha's natural eyesight was gone, he saw where Gehazi had gone and what he had done. Elisha's broken heart went with Gehazi when he chased after Naaman. He confronted Gehazi by asking him, "Is it a time to receive money?"

Gehazi is like so many of us who are ignorant of our season.

Gehazi served Elisha, who had gotten a double portion of the grace, gifting and anointing that was on Elijah. Elisha received this great gift by simply waiting on the Lord and keeping his eye on his purpose to serve the man of God. Gehazi took his eyes off his purpose and got tired of waiting. As a result of his lying and conniving, Gehazi exchanged the possibility of a double portion blessing for leprosy.

Bob Hope was admired for so many things but most of all for having "perfect timing." Many of us lack the patience to tell a joke. Instead of setting it up with the right words, we blurt out the ending too soon. Our lack of timing kills the joke. So was it with Gehazi. He lacked timing. His life had such promise and possibility but instead he forfeited it all due to his unwillingness to wait.

The message of Gehazi is simply that God has a season for everything (Ecc 3). The Bible tells us to recognize the season. Gehazi is like so many of us who are IGNORANT OF OUR SEASON.

The good news about Gehazi is that he appeared to be redeemed by having a second chance to get it right (a do-over). In Sennacherib's case God intervened by having the Syrian army "hear what sounded like the roar of a huge cavalry."

At the same time, four lepers were starving to death. They made a decision that they would go to the Syrian camp and beg for food. They reasoned that the worst thing that could happen would be their death at the hand of the Syrians. If they didn't go they would starve to death, but the Syrians had fled in fear, leaving everything behind just like Elisha had prophesied to the king.

When they arrived at the camp they found it abandoned. They began to hoard the clothes, gold and other abandoned property when they decided that they needed to go and tell the Samaritans the good news.

We don't know for sure if Gehazi is one of the four men with leprosy. However, we see him a little bit later standing next to the king, telling him about the widow whose son had been raised from the dead by Elisha. It might be that God healed Gehazi because of his do-over.

We know that kings had nothing to do with lepers. It is highly possible that Gehazi took the place of the king's chief officer who was trampled in fulfillment of Elisha's word. It is wonderful to contemplate that no matter how bad we have been, God is the author of the second chance.

Every person that has ever lived (except Jesus) has needed a do-over. I play golf once a year and enjoy it in spite of my limited skill and ability. I want a "Mulligan" on every hole. I am not there to count strokes but to have a good time. Life would be very sad if there were no second chances. The prodigal son represents a second chance. He too was unwilling to wait for his season of blessing.

Another major thing not to do when waiting for the Lord is to go without revelation. Governments and military from time immemorial have always wanted more information. They have craved "intel" so that they could make right decisions. Many bad decisions are the result of not taking the time to gather all the relevant facts.

David was a man after God's own heart but far from perfect. He was especially flawed as a father. His son Absalom stole the hearts of the people by telling them what he would do if he was king. Absalom ended up leading a revolt, forcing David and the rest of his family and those loyal to him to flee. The followers of the two men fought each other and Absalom was killed.

A man named Ahimaaz was a fast runner and part of the messenger team that carried messages from the front line to the king. He pressed Joab, David's general, to let him move in his gifting and allow him to run to King David. Joab resisted his request and said, "Why will you run since you have no news?" Nevertheless, Ahimaaz insisted that he be allowed to run to the king.

Finally, Joab told him to go ahead and run. Ahimaaz took off running and outran the official messenger sent by Joab. When he arrived in the presence of the king, he was asked what had happened to Absalom. Ahimaaz said he saw a commotion but did not know what had really happened (2 Sam 11).

Don't run without a revelation.

David told Ahimaaz to stand aside as the runner who carried the message was arriving. Of course, he told King David that Joab and his army had won a great battle. When the king asked about Absalom, the messenger said, "Would that all the king's enemies were like him – dead."

Ahimaaz moved in his gifting without any revelation. We have no anointing when we have no revelation. Too many of us try to preach, build, buy or do something else without waiting to get the revelation. Ahimaaz had a general revelation but the king wanted specifics. Like Ahimaaz, some of us want to run come what may. The blessing (and revelation) comes when we wait on the Lord. DON'T RUN WITHOUT A REVELATION.

Many of us grow impatient when God or somebody is late for an appointment. King Saul waited seven days for the prophet Samuel before stepping into the prophet/priest role of offering a sacrifice. Saul felt compelled to take action because the people were beginning to scatter. Saul was operating under conventional wisdom, which says any decision is better than no decision.

Right after Saul made this decision, Samuel showed up. Saul substituted his fears for faith and his reasoning for the commandment to wait. Like many of us, Saul was not a patient man. And like many of us, Saul's impatience led him to do something stupid (1 Sam13).

We need to bury Worry.

Waiting is a time when our fears torment us. We begin to think that we must have missed God. Every believer has gone through a time when God seems silent and distant. It's a time to stand still, pray, seek the Lord. It's a time to remind ourselves – DON'T DO SOMETHING STUPID.

The tormented Christian thinks too much and prays too little. He is a "worry-wart" – a person who habitually worries. Many years ago I was reading the obituary section in the local paper (a perverse habit to make sure that I am not dead) when I saw memorial information for "Worry Paulson." I never knew anybody named Worry, though I have known many who are world-class worriers. We need to bury Worry. Waiting is a time to confess truth and wait for Him who is Truth.

Waiting is directly connected to vision. In Habakkuk 2:1-3 the prophet challenges God's people to write the vision down, make it plain and wait for it. The Bible is full of lives that were changed or wrecked by impatience.

Moses killed the Egyptian and ended up spending forty years in the wilderness. Aaron made a golden calf and was stopped from going into the promised land. Moses struck the rock instead of speaking to it and was also stopped from going into the promised land. Abraham fathered Ishmael and there has been war between his descendents ever since.

When my wife and I owned a restaurant, we saw the difference between an experienced and inexperienced waiter. The inexperienced waiter failed to keep his eye on the customer or ask relevant questions (Soup or salad? Drinks? How would you like that cooked?).

The inexperienced waiter was inefficient in anticipating the needs of the customer and at other times failed to leave the table and let the diners eat without his hovering presence. The biggest offense was failure of the inexperienced waiter to bring the bill to the table when the customer was ready to go.

On the other hand, the experienced waiter anticipated his customer's need for water, refills, desert, condiments and the bill. The experienced waiter assisted his customer in making decisions, from appetizers to main course to dessert. The really good waiter even adjusted his personality to the customer.

God has called us to be professional waiters. Simeon was waiting for the promised Messiah when he heard the whisper of the Spirit of God. As Simeon went into the temple to meet baby Jesus, his waiting was finally over. Simeon was an old man who must have battled many fears and doubts. But something inside of Simeon said, "Wait and you will see the salvation of the Lord" (Luke 2).

John the Baptist was also a professional waiter. He had the wonderful experience of seeing the dove descend on Jesus as he water-baptized Jesus. Later when he was in prison, The Baptist began to have doubts. John sent disciples to ask Jesus if he was the Messiah.

Jesus told them to go and tell John what they saw – the lame walk and the blind see. Even professional, anointed waiters can suffer doubts.

Joseph needed to wait through many adversities in order to get the blessing promised him in two different dreams. Joseph believed that God was going to honor him and that his own family was going to bow down before him. Joseph was severely tested as his brothers sold him into slavery and then he was falsely accused of rape, locked up and forgotten. It was twenty years of waiting before the dream was fulfilled (Gen 37 -42).

The little "to" stage between the glories of God kills a lot of flesh.

Family and friends might mock you or doubt you when you share your dream. Circumstances or Satan might do everything possible to kill your dream. God says

WAIT FOR IT.

Your life seems to be on hold. It's a time when you can't do the things you need to do. You are at the mercy of God, others or circumstances. There are little everyday holds like telephone holds, traffic lights and the lines at grocery stores, gas stations and restaurants. But there are some really big holds like a difficult marriage, a dead end job, debt pressure, health problems or unfulfilling ministry.

Abraham heard God speak clearly that his descendents were going to be like the sand of the sea (Gen 12). Time passed and Abraham (and Sarah too) aged. From his perspective time was running out. Their lives were on hold. Sarah was past the childbearing age and even Viagra would not help brother Abraham.

We birth an Ishmael whenever we grow impatient and take the matter or circumstance into our own hands.

God does not wear a wristwatch. His ways are not our ways. He is never early and never late even though He is often accused of being late (e.g. Mary and Martha when their brother Lazarus died). The Bible says from glory to glory God is changing us.

The little "to" stage between the glories of God kills a lot of flesh. It was during this "to" stage that Abraham and Sarah yielded to man's greatest temptation – to help God out.

Abraham and Sarah started to think how they could help fulfill the word spoken by God (great self-help Christians). Here is Hagar the little maid of Sarah who could be the surrogate mom and help fulfill the prophecy spoken over Abraham.

The result is Ishmael, son of Abraham and Hagar and father of the Arab nations. Ishmael's name has become synonymous for do-it-yourself Christianity. We birth an Ishmael whenever we grow impatient and take the matter or circumstance into our own hands.

The temptation to help God out is not born in faith but in fear that God will not do what He said that He would do. Sin is simply doing that which is against God's will. His will is written clearly in the Bible. The Old Testament sets out the law so that man will realize that he can never be good enough to get to heaven or God without humbling himself and calling on the name of the Lord.

Abraham and Sarah followed a recipe for destruction. They grew impatient and yielded to the temptation to help God out. They took God's promise and mixed it generously with man's method. After nine months of cooking, out comes Ishmael. It all started because their lives were on hold.

I never like it when the airplane pilot comes on the speaker and announces, "Ladies and gentlemen, we have been placed in a holding pattern. I will let you know when we are cleared for landing." After a long trip of ten or fifteen hours in the air, I want out of the plane so bad that I can almost taste the ground. What can I do? Should I stand up and demand that they land now because I am tired and do not want my life to go into a holding pattern? Should I march up and knock on the pilot's door with my demand? I'm sure the sky marshall would put me in a worse holding pattern.

There are many reasons why God might put you on hold. My wife taught our children a little song written by

Frank Hernandez and Sherry Saunders called *Patience* from *The Music Machine*. It goes like this:

Have patience, have patience
Don't be in such a hurry.
When you get impatient,
You only start to worry.
Remember, remember.
That God is patient too.
And think of all the times when
Others have to wait for you.

Patience is a virtue that seems to grow on some people's trees more than others. Unfortunately for all the Type A personalities of the world, God puts us on hold to grow some patience on our fruit tree.

Sometimes our lives are on hold because God is getting ready to take us in a new direction. God is allowing a pause in our lives so that we can take care of a few things before He pushes the play button. Most of us men are experts on running our television remote control clickers.

We know how to pause so that we can run to the bathroom, take a phone call or go to the refrigerator. We put the program on hold until we are ready to push the play button. Sometimes God is doing the same thing in our lives so that we can take care of some housekeeping before our lives move into the next busy season.

During times that our lives are on hold, God increases our sensitivity to His timing. It is a time to reaffirm who is Lord of our lives. Is it our daytimer or His heavenly timing? It is a time when God is bringing us into unity.

God gives perfect peace to those whose mind is fixed on Him. As a life-long visionary I have a wandering and wondering mind. Holding times force me to refocus my life, dreams, hopes and ambitions on Him. I need to remove the clutter and irrelevant things so that there is nothing between His glory and me. He must increase and I must decrease.

When your life is on hold, make a decision to refocus on the Lord. Maybe you add a little more Word, prayer and fasting as you are actively waiting on the Lord to take your life off hold. Leave a message on God's voice mail and trust that He will get back to you (Ps 37).

Avoid the temptation to grumble, blame others, become resentful, compare yourself to others or covet their ministry. I like the old song *Jesus on the Mainline* that says, "Just call Him up and tell Him what you want." My wife and brother hate that song as they think it's bad theology. Maybe it is, but one thing I have learned is that God hears the cry of His children.

God is allowing a pause in our lives so that we can take care of a few things before He pushes the play button.

I am always giving my wife a bad time, as her Methodist heritage demands a little more labor from the person making the call. My Catholic background has no problem with the theology of calling on the Lord during our time of distress.

Even in the natural, Cathy is reluctant to bother others with a problem but resorts to trying to figure things out herself. After over forty years of marriage, we really know each other but still approach life and problems differently. To her credit, she is far more saintly and patient.

Every day I think we should "call Him up and tell Him what we want." I want you, Lord. I want Your plan, Your peace, Your blessing, Your will. If you don't get the Lord on the line, leave your message and hang up. God has your number.

In the movie *Bruce Almighty*, actor Jim Carrey played a man named Bruce who fantasized about what he would do if he were God. Suddenly God (or was it Morgan Freeman?) allowed Bruce to become God for a day. Bruce was overwhelmed with the problems of the world and all the people sending their prayer requests. He did not have enough time to read and analyze each request so he decided to say yes to everybody. This created more chaos and unhappiness for those who called on the name of the Almighty.

When I lost my race for Attorney General of Montana, one of my friends modified a popular country song called *Making the Best of a Bad Situation*. I laughed so hard that I almost cried. If our life is on hold, we need to make the best of a bad situation.

Our impatience is not going to hurry God. Kert, the Open Arms church administrator, used to be an administrator for UCLA. As the overseer of UCLA food service, the football players pressed him to bring the pizza or other food NOW.

A key to receiving God's blessing is to wait with open hands and an open heart.

Kert said, "I told them it was going to be even longer now that they were pushing me. If they wanted it to be even slower, all they needed to do was keep pushing and I would slow down even more."

While I don't think that God is like my friend who went even slower when he was pushed, I think that God wants His perfect work to be accomplished in our lives during a holding time. Isaiah reminds us that those who wait (or are in a holding pattern) on the Lord will renew their strength.

Waiting is one of the hardest things we do. It is not a passive time of twiddling our thumbs, but actively listening, praying and pursuing the Lord. A key to receiving God's blessing is to wait with open hands and an open heart. He will fill both your hands and your hearts.

10

The Benefits of Criticism

Position for Blessing - Embrace Criticism

THE PATHWAY TO THE PROMISED LAND for Israel, as the people marched out of Egypt, was not a straight path. It was interrupted by their fears and their complaints. They grumbled their way towards the Promised Land only to be denied because of their unbelief in the power and sufficiency of God.

The whole world knows a bit about God but do they really know God? The blessing of the Lord comes from really knowing God – not in knowing about God. Like Moses, we need some face-time with the great I AM.

For you and me to get to our own Promised Land, we must overcome grumblings from within and giants from without. I have found one of the best methods to help me get to the Promised Land is to listen and learn from the criticism of others. If nobody is criticizing you, it's because you aren't doing anything.

The Bible is about God, man and circumstances. Peter and the disciples told Jesus that eating His body and drinking His blood was a "hard saying" (Jn 6:60). Some things in life are hard to be understood. If we are going to get the blessing that God intends for us, we have to deal with some hard, difficult things.

David was described as a man after God's heart and yet he had to come through many intense problems. One of the hardest things David needed to endure was constant criticism from everyone. If we want to be like David, we need to endure criticism. David's acceptance and integration of the criticism is one of his great secrets to becoming a man after God's heart.

David's older brother Eliab accused David of thinking too highly of himself. David ignored the criticism because he was focused on becoming a giant killer. Criticism can make or break us. David refused to be deterred by the criticism of his brother. It caused him to become even more determined to fulfill his destiny as a giant killer.

If we want to be like David, we need to endure criticism.

David was almost stoned by his best friends after thieves stole their families and possessions at Ziklag. The key to everything was David keeping his mouth shut in the face of overwhelming criticism. God restored all that was lost. The Bible says that if I hold my peace, the Lord will fight my battles (Ex 14:14).

“I think we should change the name of the church,” I announced to my wife one day.

“Why would we do that? Open Arms is a great name for the people that we have. It’s consistent with the mission that God has given us to ‘give hope and help to the brokenhearted,’” Cathy argued.

“You’re right,” I confessed. “But every time I go to the church and see the folks that we have lost to drugs, alcohol or the street, I need to encourage myself in the Lord.”

“That’s true, but what does that have to do with changing the name of the church?” asked Cathy.

“I feel just like David who had to encourage himself in the Lord at Ziklag,” I explained. “Every time I go to Open Arms (Ziklag) I have to encourage myself in the Lord.”

Ziklag was both a high and low point for David. Ultimately, our lives are all about finding the face of the Lord in the midst of our grief and sorrow. There is no substitute for the still, small voice of God in the midst of our pain and confusion. Perhaps, the lesson learned at Ziklag was what carried David through so many criticisms and setbacks.

After David was set in as King of Israel, he went to fetch the ark of God. As he was bringing the ark to Jerusalem, David danced with all his might as an act of worship. His wife, Michal, looked out a window and despised him for being so open before all the people.

We used to sing a song about David’s response. Some of the words of the song were, “I’ll be yet more vile, said David unto Michal.” We sang as we danced with all our might. David’s answer to criticism was to worship.

Later David committed adultery with beautiful Bathsheba which led to her pregnancy and murder of her husband Uriah. God sent the prophet to criticize and pronounce judgment on David for his sin.

David did not lie or deny but immediately humbled himself through fasting and prayer, hoping that God might change his mind and not allow the death of his child. When the child died, David cleaned himself up, sat and worshipped the Lord. Again, David positioned himself for future blessing by responding instead of reacting to the criticism brought by the prophet.

Rather than dealing with the criticisms of his disloyal son Absalom, David ignored them, believing that they would just disappear. Instead, David lost his kingship for a season and almost lost his life. Criticisms cannot always be minimized or ignored if you want to hold on to your power and life.

What do you do when somebody throws rocks (or criticisms) at you? As David and his loyalists were fleeing certain death at the hands of Absalom, a man named Shimei walked alongside them throwing rocks and cursing David. Shimei was a relative of deceased King Saul and blamed David for his problems. One of David's military leaders wanted to go shut him up, but David told him to leave him alone as God might have sent him.

Criticisms cannot always be minimized or ignored....

David's response to Shimei's criticism teaches us how to deal with critics. First, keep your mouth shut. Don't argue, explain, justify, defend or attack. David kept his mouth shut even though his flesh wanted to cry out, clarify, defend, blame or accuse. Jesus is the ultimate example of one who kept His mouth shut when He stood before His critics.

Secondly, endure the criticism. It's a time to listen, pray and process. If you don't tell your noisy soul to shut up, you will never be able to get through to the other end of the criticism.

Third, stop your family and friends from picking up an offense. To the one who is hurt goes the grace of healing. Over the years I have been criticized many times (both justly and unjustly). My wife and family want to get out and defend me. The defense offered by family and friends is to attack the other side.

"Who do they think they are? They aren't perfect either," asserts the family defender.

Fourth, believe God will vindicate you. It pleases the Lord when we are falsely accused, as nothing burns up the old man faster or more completely than false accusation. Consciously choose humility over anything and everything else. The way up is down.

Overreacting to a criticism is usually evidence that the criticism is partially true.

The natural man does not like it when somebody throws rocks at him. He wants to get his own rocks or something bigger. Everything screams, "Fight back!" Yet, the still, small voice of God whispers, "Dead men have no rights." God says if you hold your peace, He will fight your battles.

Shakespeare once wrote in Hamlet, "The lady doth protest too much, me thinks." Overreacting to a criticism is usually evidence that the criticism is partially true.

Joab was David's very flawed general. He killed innocent men and was the man who drove a javelin through the body of Absalom even though the king ordered that they go easy on Absalom. Joab was one of the king's closest advisers. He was known as the go-to and get-it-done guy. When the king woke up one morning and decided that he wanted to count the people of Israel, Joab told him in the strongest words possible that it was not a good idea.

Joab criticized the king for even thinking of counting the people, as he knew that this was a statement of unbelief. The king dug in his heals and ordered him to do it anyway. I think that David just didn't like Joab even though he was a gifted man. When Joab said don't do it, David got stubborn and wanted to do it even more.

Some people do not know how to give counsel so they give criticism instead.

This was a costly mistake by David and ultimately caused a confrontation with a prophet and the loss of life by the people. When we get stubborn, we lose the benefit that God wants to give us through the criticism.

There are many specific benefits to receiving criticism. One of the chief benefits of criticism is that it allows us to receive the counsel of others. Over the years of working with people, I have used a small phrase that I heard from Accelerated Christian Education - "Praise publicly. Correct privately." Now it is not without limitations.

We know that Paul criticized Peter publicly for his unacceptable and legalistic behavior in Galatia. The first reaction when somebody criticizes us is to draw a protective covering over ourselves as quickly as we can. We throw on our bulletproof Teflon vest as we pull our gun, prepared to shoot back.

Some people do not know how to give counsel so they give criticism instead. Pontius Pilate said, "What is truth?" The critic might have been out of order, over the top and disrespectful. However, what is truth? Can you control your old nature enough to process what you are hearing?

As a pastor for over thirty years, I have been criticized by many. Christianity and "churchianity" are team sports similar to basketball where the fans have an opinion over every whistle blown by the referee (aka the pastor). Clever people criticize you by asking a question, "Why did you do that?" Implicit in the question is, "You are wrong," or, "How could you be so dumb?"

Thank God for people who can see my blind spots...

During these times, I force myself not to react but listen hard for the still, small voice of God. What is He saying? Unless it is so clear that the criticism is nothing but an attack of the enemy, I teFll them, "I will "pray about that." This is not some super-spiritual stall but a desire to know what God is saying. Remember, GOD WILL LEAD YOU THE EASIEST WAY YOU LET HIM. Maybe God sent Charlie Critic because you were stubborn or proud.

Another great benefit of criticism is that it allows us to see our blind spots. I can't see the back of my head. I don't know if my hair is sticking straight out or if I have some other problem. "I got your back" is a commitment of love and loyalty. Thank God for the family and friends who "got my back" and show it by sharing timely criticisms.

Mark Twain reportedly said, "Your best friend is not the person who tells you what you want to hear but what you need to hear." Thank God for people who can see my blind spots and are willing to be misunderstood (and possibly attacked by my old nature) but still go forward and share their criticism.

When you are criticized, it's a time for you to decrease and for Christ to increase. I am convinced that people are not turned off by Christ but by many of His disciples. The Kingdom of God is so different than the kingdom of man. You hit a man, he hits you back. You take a man's coat, he sues you.

But, this is not the way it is done in God's Kingdom. He says, "Turn the other cheek, walk the second mile, give them the shirt off your back." If somebody reviles you, don't revile back. All of this means less of me and more of Him.

Another great benefit of criticism is that it leads us to repentance. Many of us are insensitive and oblivious to the thoughts, concerns, and feelings of others. Criticism sensitizes us, develops empathy in us and leads us to a place of repentance.

A dead man has no rights, no opinions and no reaction to criticism...

To repent means you change your mind, you go in a different direction. Repentance needs to be a good friend. The world hates proud and loves humble (unless you are Donald Trump).

Repentance is connected to humble. We used to sing the little chorus, "Humble yourself in the sight of the Lord and He will lift you up."

Closely connected to all of this is the principle of dying to self. When somebody criticizes you, it is like a doctor testing to see if you are alive. This is one of Dr. Jesus' favorite methods to check your spiritual death status. If you are still alive and kicking, Dr. Jesus might encourage you to give it up!

Paul said to die is gain. Criticism is both a test of whether you are still alive and kicking as well as a method intended to help kill the old man. A dead man has no rights, no opinions and no reaction to criticism (or compliments either).

Criticism encourages humility. Many of us have eaten our fill of humble pie. A good response to criticism might be to say simply, "Thank you for sharing that concern. I never thought about it before but will do so now." I am so grateful for both my friends and my foes. Humility takes the words out of the mouths of our enemies and leaves them speechless.

One of the greatest benefits of criticism is that it allows God to vindicate us. Instead of arguing with a fool and thereby becoming a fool, it is best to keep our yap shut and let the Lord separate the wheat from the chaff. As believers we only have one master. He has set us free from the life-ruining, impossible task of being a people-pleaser.

"If I hold my peace, the Lord will fight my battles." God is the one who raises and lowers us and He does it through our response (or reaction) to criticism. Our Heavenly Father is the unseen listener to every conversation. He is more concerned about your heart than your feelings. When it coincides with His long-term plan, God will lift you up just like He did with Joseph in Egypt.

God is looking for Proverbs 27 Christians. His Word says that "open rebuke is better than secret love." Criticism is a testimony that you really love or care for a person. Apathy and indifference is the response we give to strangers. When we truly love a person, we risk being misunderstood and tell them what we really think.

Many of us have strong opinions about sports, politics, music, government and a thousand other things. However, we are a collection of couch potatoes grumbling and criticizing but never picking up a phone or writing a letter. All the silent seething and pontificating do nothing to change the circumstance. However, if we call, write or confront, it is possible that circumstances might change.

"Faithful are the wounds of a friend," says Proverbs 27. Your best friend does not cut you up with rumors, gossip and whispering. Real friends get in your face. They tell you what they think even if you don't like it.

Too many take a pass as they hate confrontation and conflict. Instead, they justify their unbiblical response by saying, "He never listens. It would not make any difference." Such a conclusion is a lie to cover up cowardly conduct. Galatians 6:1 says, "If a brother is overtaken in a fault, you who are spiritual confront them in a spirit of meekness considering yourself lest you also be tempted."

Real friends get in your face.

Proverbs 27 says, "As iron sharpens iron so does a man sharpen the countenance of his friend." I have had many sword battles with those believers whose conviction and courage were strong enough to get out of their comfort zone and confront.

Care enough to confront. The people that we hate are not the ones we confront, argue and criticize but the ones that we ignore. By ignoring somebody we are telling them, "You do not mean enough to me to even fight with."

Criticism is not easy to receive but is as necessary as prayer. God does not chastise the devil's children but He does spank His own. An aftershave commercial on television shows a man pouring some aftershave on his hand and slapping his face. Then he says, "Thank you, I needed that." When somebody slaps you unexpectedly with criticism, God is not surprised. He knew from the foundation of time that this critical conversation was going to occur.

Criticism is such a key to being blessed. Our flesh cries out for protection and justification when we are criticized but our spirit simply says, "Thank you, I needed that." A sign of maturity is our ability and willingness to hear the bad and the ugly. We all like to hear, "Well done."

We will never become the man or woman of God that He has intended us to be until we learn to receive criticism without reacting. We need to thank God for people loving enough and courageous enough to speak the truth (as they understand it) into our lives. Even if they get it wrong, the criticism can be a stepping-stone to the next blessing God has reserved for us.

11

Forgiveness is a Decision

Position for Blessing - Practice Forgiveness

THE BIBLE TELLS US, "Taste and see. The Lord is good." When people come across a Christian, they get a free "taste test" to decide if they want to buy into Christianity. Too often the potential believer gets a bitter taste that sends them in another direction.

They taste the bitter, unforgiving spirit of a believer who is carrying a grudge or has issues. They have come into contact with an ambassador of unforgiveness rather than an ambassador of the one who hung on a cross and said, "Father forgive them, they know not what they do."

The essence of Christianity is about grace and forgiveness. To forgive means to cancel a debt or set somebody free. When we forgive, we make a decision to put something behind us. According to Micah 7:19, once we repent God puts our sins into the depths of the sea never more to be seen or remembered. Forgiveness is not something you earn but something that is freely given.

Many have tried to define forgiveness. The Eskimo word for forgiveness is "issumagijoujungnainermik." It means not being able to think about it anymore.

A little boy was asked if he knew what forgiveness was. He said, "Sure, forgiveness is the odor that a flower gives when trampled on." How many of us can apply either of these great definitions when we are hurt and offended? What do you smell like when somebody tramples on you?

Forgiveness is the heart of the Lord's Prayer – "Forgive us our trespasses as we forgive others." Jesus understood that forgiveness is a major problem for mankind. He says, "If you have anything against anyone, lay your gift at the altar and go to them."

Forgiveness is the odor that a flower gives when trampled on.

Bitterness hurts everybody but especially the person holding on to the grudge. It's a cancer that steals your joy long after the offender has forgotten (if they were even aware to begin with) what happened.

The devil is the god of unforgiveness. He has a clicker in his hand and is constantly hitting the replay button until the whole issue is burned into your memory bank. Only God, through His grace, can clean our hard drive. This requires humility. Holding an offense is an open invitation to the devil to bring other spirits that are equally offensive as unforgiveness. Some of these spirits include bitterness, violence, accusation and gossip.

I have been asked by those who have been hurt badly if they "have to forgive." I assure them that they do not have to forgive. They don't need to get saved either, as Hell is always an option! If they have cancer, they don't need to see a medical doctor or get treatment. Holding a grudge is a sin just like adultery, gluttony, pride, stubbornness, and the rest of the self-centered sins.

If you have been offended and are wrestling with a spirit of bitterness, get over it. Forgiveness is both a decision and a process. It requires you to identify with Christ who suffered and died for our sins. God expects us to pray for our enemies. It requires faith and obedience that this is the will of God. One who holds unforgiveness gets to relive the original pain day after day.

Forgiveness is a process more than an event. It frees us from the bondage of bitterness and releases others to forgive. My dad used to say, "Do it to me once, shame on you. Do it to me twice, shame on me." However, God does not say that. He says forgive seventy times seven. You are never a sucker if you have embraced the foolishness of the cross.

Many of us grew up with some form of homespun wisdom that told us to keep track of our enemies. Richard Nixon had an enemies list of people that hurt him. Most of us have a list of people that we want to avoid because they have hurt us. We pretend we don't see them or walk down the other side of the street.

Forgiveness is both a decision and a process.

The benefits of forgiveness include protection from Satan's inroads. It allows us to become mature, normal

Christians moving past the offense. It needs to be freely given, not legalistically demanded. It is an act of love, an opportunity not an obligation. It is what makes us Christians.

Jesus is our hero, our Savior and our example. Jesus said, "The works that I do shall you do also." We are called to die to self (like Jesus did in Gethsemane) so that we can forgive others and live for Christ. Jesus is in the forgiveness business. And, we need to be in the same business.

What do you do when you have been hurt? We have all been hurt. When Jesus told his disciples that they needed to forgive, they said, "Increase our faith." It takes faith to believe in God and faith to forgive.

There are four common responses (or reactions) to being hurt. The first and most common response is anger. God's Word admonishes us not to let the sun go down while we are angry (Eph 4:26). Whoever is angry is in danger (Matt 5:22). We are told to "make no friendship with an angry man." God wants to protect us from catching the spirit of anger by hanging out with angry people.

Many years ago, I felt the Lord speak to me to limit my friendship with a man who was known for his fits of anger. It was so painful for me to tell my friend that I could have nothing more to do with him because he was an angry man. I was trying to be obedient to the Lord in rebuking my friend. He did not like or agree with what I said to him, but he changed, and God restored our special friendship.

A second major response to being hurt is to find ways of getting even. We console ourselves with the Old Testament scripture, "An eye for an eye, a tooth for a tooth." God says, "Vengeance is mine" (Deut 32:35). The Bible says that when we love our enemies we are putting coals of fire on them.

Benjamin Franklin understood forgiveness. Franklin spoke with great wisdom when he said:

> "Doing an injury puts you below your enemy; revenging makes you but even with him; forgiving sets you above him."

I remember a sign that I saw on a wall of a bar (BC – before Christ). It said, "Great minds talk about ideas. Medium minds talk about current events. Small minds talk about people." Unforgivers are always caught up talking about people.

If you want to get even (or get over) with your enemies, do what the Bible says – forgive them. Vindication is a first cousin to vengeance. David prayed in Psalms, "Let my vindication come from Your presence" (Ps 17:2). David sought to be vindicated through God's righteousness and strength.

Many years ago I was interviewing a man from our church who wanted to be presented for prayer and prophecy at special spiritual meetings called a presbytery. I asked the man what he hoped God would do in his life. He said, "I want God to vindicate me."

If you want to get even (or get over) with your enemies, do what the Bible says – forgive them.

This man had caused untold problems in the church. People had marked him as someone to avoid. He refused counsel and was a first rate hardhead. As the man was presented for ministry, the lead prophet came to me and said that he had the word "troublemaker."

Normally, these words are shared privately, but I felt God wanted the non-vindication to be spoken publicly, so I told the prophet to speak openly what he had. The prophet said, "You are a troublemaker but God wants to make you a peacemaker."

There was no vindication for our brother because God was trying to shine His light of truth on his inward parts. He rejected the word, quit the church and ended up divorcing his wife. I pray that he became the peacemaker God called him to be.

A third area common to those who have been hurt is to demand restitution. This is a kinder version of the eye-for-an-eye method. Restitution is not always possible, as the person might be judgment-proof or dead and buried. The law uses money as restitution.

As a lawyer/litigator I have counseled hundreds of people who have been hurt. Oftentimes, the best counsel is to walk away and forgive them. The legal process is long and expensive and there is no guarantee that they will win. I used to have a t-shirt that said, "TALK IS CHEAP UNTIL YOU HIRE A LAWYER."

There is no real healing until the hurt and injury is put behind you. My sister had a dead battery explode in her face, causing her to lose an eye. Although she had to go through an arduous healing process, the real healing did not take place until the lawsuit was over.

A fourth way that many deal with unforgiveness is to minimize the extent of the hurt. They pretend that they don't hurt or that they have forgiven the offender. Minimizers are lying to themselves and others. When he was painting *The Last Supper*, Leonardo da Vinci painted the face of another artist into the face of Judas Iscariot.

It's rightly stated that, "You cannot at one and the same time be painting the features of Christ into your life, and painting another face with enmity and hatred."

God's time-tested solution for any and all hurt is to forgive, pray and bless. There is only one reason that people become angry, bitter and unforgiving – they are alive to self. God says, "Except a seed fall in the ground and die, it abides alone" (Jn 12:20-26). Out of death comes life and multiplication. You are dead when you don't fight back.

Jesus died emotionally and spiritually in the Garden of Gethsemane. He said, "My soul is exceedingly sorrowful even to death" (Matt 26:36-46). Jesus struggled with the crucifixion and looked for an alternative. After sweating blood, Jesus said, "Not my will, but thy will be done." It is death when we give up our own will and fully embrace the will of another.

Jesus died emotionally and spiritually in the Garden of Gethsemane.

Christian author Gene Edwards has written many books challenging believers to die to self and live for Christ. In one of the strongest statements that I have ever read, Edwards said:

> "The cross seeks out man's desire to not suffer and man's furious commitment to never lose, and his screaming logic that he is not wrong."

Many times in my life, I wanted to be right more than I wanted to be reconciled. Crucifixions reveal and destroy. In the end we have to remember that every crucifixion is about death.

Paul shows us the way to be dead to self in Romans 6. Positionally and theologically we have died to sin when we come to Christ. The Word says that we have been baptized into His death. We are buried with Him and are no longer slaves to sin. Unforgiveness is the sign of an incomplete death. We need to reckon the old man as dead and buried.

The Bible is full of people who have altered their lives by anger and bitterness. Cain was bitter and unforgiving when God accepted the offering of Abel and refused his offering. His anger and unforgiveness led to murder. Moses got angry at the people he was leading and struck the rock instead of speaking to it. Absalom did not forgive his brother who raped his sister. Ultimately he did the same thing as Cain and killed his brother.

Most of us get angry and throw temper tantrums, honk the horn or wave the middle finger (I don't do that just in case you are curious), but we don't kill anybody. Road rage (or parking lot rage) is common. Man has come up with various solutions on how to "manage your anger."

Anger management classes have become big business. We are encouraged to vent, use an anger mantra, keep an anger calendar and practice other methods designed to control the demon within.

God challenges us to be slow to speak, quick to hear and slow to anger. If we want to position ourselves for His blessing, we need to free ourselves from every bitter spirit.

Jonah was like many of us. When God told him to go and do something, he ran away. God trapped him with a storm, tossed him into the sea and swallowed him with a whale.

Then God gave Jonah a second chance to take the message to Nineveh. After Jonah gave Nineveh the message, the entire city repented. God was gracious, compassionate and forgiving. Jonah became angry because he did not want God to forgive the people of Nineveh.

Forgiveness is a decision. It is learned behavior that comes from knowing the heart of God. The Bible says that God is love. Forgiveness is a direct act of love. It is not sterile and disconnected to our feelings. The feelings of hurt must follow the decision of forgiveness.

Actors and actresses must stay in character when they are playing a part. They need to own the role and not ever forget that this is what they have been called to be. Many years ago the manager of our personnel business exhorted me, "I will take care of this. Go do what you do best. Go love somebody."

Blessing or bitterness? You and I get to choose.

As Christians, we need to stay in character. Our calling as sons and daughters of God is to love. The first commandment is to love God and the second is to love our neighbor as ourselves.

Forgiveness and love go hand in hand. You are out of character (and a poor Christian witness) when you fail to forgive whosoever God puts in your life. There is only one unforgiveable sin – blaspheming the Holy Spirit. You and I are not the Holy Spirit.

God has created us in His image and likeness. His plan is to lead us to a life of blessing. One of the biggest hurdles that must be overcome is bitterness. We have all been hurt by people and circumstances.

From the cross, the only innocent man who ever lived cries out for the world to hear, "Father, forgive them for they know not what they do." If we are going to live the life God intended, we need to become a world-class lover/forgiver.

Blessing or bitterness? You and I get to choose. We can't have both. It's either/or.

12

Who's Your Paul? Who's Your Timothy?

Position for Blessing - Be a Mentor and a Disciple

Somebody once said, "A fool never learns from his mistakes; a wise man learns from his own mistakes; and a genius learns from the mistakes of others." I know that I have been a fool many times, and I have been wise once or twice, but my deepest desire is to be a genius.

We need to learn from others - parents, teachers, coaches, writers, friends, spouse, etc. The Bible says, "Some are ever learning and never coming to the knowledge of the truth." God has a special system to teach us right from wrong, how to make a decision, and how to avoid making mistakes. It is called discipleship or mentoring.

Mentoring is more than an academic exercise where you read something and attempt to apply it. Paul referred to Timothy as "my own son in the faith." Paul was a father, teacher, authority, guide and coach to Timothy, who was a son, student, submitted one, disciple and follower. All over the world this special relationship is reproduced.

The essence of discipleship/mentoring is relationship. This is more than just a friendship. The disciple needs to give the mentor freedom to speak into his life while the mentor needs to exercise this freedom as a special call. The goal of discipleship is more than trying to produce a trophy.

The primary purpose is reproduction. Paul admonished Timothy, "You have often heard me teach. Now I want you to tell these same things to followers who can be trusted to tell others" (2 Tim 2:2 CEV).

Jesus broke the mold of the rabbis by calling His own disciples rather than vice-versa. Paul chose Timothy and Silas rather than Mark. Moses chose Joshua as well as the seventy elders. Elijah chose Elisha. Leaders are assisted by the Holy Spirit in deciding who to pick for mentoring or ministry. When they gathered to pray and fast, the Holy Spirit said, "Separate Barnabas and Saul for the work unto which I have called them" (Acts 13:2).

Jesus stated clearly, "You did not choose me. I chose you and sent you out to produce fruit" (Jn 15:16). We are chosen, called and commissioned by Jesus just like the first disciples. You can never become all that God wants you to be unless you are a disciple. There is no magic formula for making disciples.

Training disciples is not a cookie cutter assembly line. It is an apprenticeship that is full of the usual mess that happens when human beings interact. The Bible says,

"Where there are no oxen, the stall is clean." Discipleship is messy. In his book *Called and Committed*, Watson says:

> "Jesus shared His life with His disciples. He identified Himself fully with them and made Himself vulnerable by opening His heart to them. Part of His great attraction lay in the fact that His love was so real and that others sensed intuitively that they could trust Him. There was no duplicity about Him. His transparent openness and integrity to others showed a quality of loving that they had not known before."

Disciple-makers need to be like Jesus. They need to be blameless, willing to spend and be spent, laying down their life for their disciples. The mentor gives up privacy and comfort because he is committed to helping the disciple grow in grace and knowledge.

During my time pastoring in Helena, Montana one of my faithful Timothys would often just drop in on Sunday afternoon. Our conversation was not very profound.

"Hi. What's happening?" I asked as I opened the door for Randy to come inside.

"Nothing much. I just wanted to drop by and visit," answered my friend/disciple.

"How's everything on the home front? Any problems with Penny or the kids?" I asked.

"No problems. Just the usual stuff."

We would sit and visit about little or nothing. Oh, there were times of discussion about doctrine, church discipline, vision and everything else pertaining to the walk of faith.

However, most discipleship happens when you spend time together.

Character and values are "caught, not taught." The disciples were with Jesus. I envision them sitting around a campfire talking about the pressures and challenges of feeding the 4,000 or healing the sick. True discipleship (and real shepherding) is done with the heart more than the head or the voice.

Discipleship is more about impartation than information. Disciples were to walk behind their teacher so that they could catch his spirit. Paul said, "You know my manner of life." True discipleship is much more than academic study and information transfer, it is about imparting a manner of life.

Character and values are "caught, not taught."

Mentors are committed to persevere until the disciple has assimilated the character and values of Christ. God is more concerned about His life within us than our eschatology, hermeneutics and theology. Jesus had no formal curriculum, classroom or syllabus but simply called His disciples to be with Him.

Discipleship is not unique to Christianity. The Pharisees sent their disciples to ensnare Jesus (Matt 22:16). John the Baptist had his disciples as did Moses. Even the cults have disciples.

A disciple is different than a Christian in the same sense that a soldier is different from a factory worker. Both are Christians and citizens but God has called us to more than just biding our time waiting for the Lord to come back for us. All great men of God were disciples.

Many years ago, I was visiting with a young pastor who wanted to better understand how he could motivate people to get involved in his church. I told him that church growth experts have determined that people come to churches because of relationship and they leave because they don't like the main guy. It begins and ends with the pastor. He needs to be an example (whose faith follow) of everything that he wants others to be or do (1 Tim 4:12). Too many leaders want to be like parents and tell people, "Do as I say, not as I do."

It does not work like that. We teach part by what we say, more by what we do, and most by what we are. The Genesis principle is that everything reproduces after its own kind. In his *Basic Youth Conflicts Seminar,* Bill Gothard said, "Whatever you do in moderation, your children will do in excess."

A leader needs to lead by example in every area that he wants to reproduce. He gets his hands dirty by sweeping floors, moving chairs, cleaning toilets and sweating alongside those he wants to disciple. Jesus said, "If you want to be great in God's Kingdom, you need to be the servant of all."

We teach part by what we say, more by what we do, and most by what we are.

If you have a relationship, you speak up. You do not worry about being misunderstood. You worry about being heard. Relationship requires stepping on toes. It is a two-way street. Don't expect to mentor somebody without getting some feedback which will be both positive and negative. Indifference is a sign that you have no relationship.

A good mentor is a visionary. He does not just see what is, but what God wants to do in the life of a disciple. Motivation occurs when there are clearly defined, attainable goals. If a leader does not have a vision for the people that he is shepherding, he cannot help them. Any fool can see the problem but it takes a prophetic mentor to see the solution.

The mentor needs to touch the disciple emotionally by avoiding plasticity and superficiality. A good mentor touches the palate of his disciple so that the words of love and wisdom are swallowed and assimilated. Labels like "brother or sister" oftentimes are shallow put-offs that push people away.

Any fool can see the problem.

Mentors need to be patient, as people will work for their goals more than your goals. As a leader it is important to discover the goals of those you lead. Manipulation and intimidation are the methods of the world. God does not want mentors to become puppeteers pulling the strings of their puppets.

In his famous book, *The Prince and the Discourses*, Machiavelli states, "It is better to be feared than loved if you cannot be both." Machiavelli taught that people will continue to do what you want if they fear you, but will stop if their motivation is love.

Machiavelli represents the wisdom of man but not the wisdom of God. God is not in the business of manipulation and intimidation. He wants to lead us by His spirit. We can balk, stop or refuse to follow whenever we want as He has given us His free will.

When we lead others, we need to capture their imagination with the vision of the Lord. We should be passionate about being both a Paul and a Timothy. Passion means to feel strongly for something. It's what you live for, sacrifice and die for. It's the thing that moves you emotionally more than anything else.

God says that He will spit the lukewarm out of His mouth. Lukewarm people try to please everybody but in the end please nobody. They are not passionate about anything. God challenges us to do everything to the glory of God.

In my life I have had three major passions – politics, business and the church. I have found that politics is about power. Growing up in Montana, I thought that my destiny was in politics. I was a candidate, campaign manager, party officer, convention delegate, worker and giver. When I came to Christ, I put politics on the altar as my "Isaac."

I still feel passionate about politics, politicians and political issues. I love to invite politicians to Open Arms to share their vision and allow us to pray for them. It does not matter whether they are a believers or not, Democrats or Republicans – they can all sense the presence of the Lord as we pray for them.

Lukewarm people try to please everybody but in the end please nobody.

While politics is about power, business is all about profit. I love business people and have thoroughly enjoyed listening to them share their vision for their business. Instead of hunting, fishing, golfing or spending my time in some other hobby, my hobby has been business. I still love business and business people but need to do it with some moderation as it is not the primary call of God on my life.

My chief passion is the church, which is all about God. While politics is about power and business is about profit, the church is about love. God loves the church and through it loves the world. God is coming back for the church, not the political parties, governments or businesses, no matter how good or righteous they might appear. Our Father God sent His only begotten Son to die for the church.

I love to read or hear about the turning point of a man's life. Jacob had a turning point when he came face to face with God. During this struggle, Jacob refused to give up until he got a word from God to be blessed and protected.

Mentors need to have a "yes face."

It reminds me of a story about a man who came to the Potomac River in the 1800s and asked if it was passable even though the river was close to flooding. One man said yes and invited the stranger to get on his horse and ride across the river.

When they reached the other side, somebody asked the stranger how he had the audacity to ask President Jefferson to take him across the river. The stranger said, "I didn't know it was President Jefferson. He was the only one with a YES FACE."

Mentors need to have a "yes face." We cannot disciple others if we are little more than semi-professional critics waiting to unload our negative opinion. Our disciples need to catch our spirit. We need a can-do spirit that challenges our disciples to believe that they can be changed into the image and likeness of God.

After losing the election for Montana Attorney General, I needed to know if God wanted me to go at it again just like His people did in Judges 19. My wife and I talked about it and decided that I needed to spend some time fasting and praying.

So I went and checked into the Motel 6 (what can I say except that I'm cheap) so I could hear His voice on the future.

As I knelt and prayed, I found that my stomach was growling so loudly that I could not hear His voice. I decided to order a pizza, watch the news and call my wife. After eating my fill, watching the news, and talking to my wife, it was time to go back to my knees and restart my fast. I was on my knees for just a few minutes when I heard the Lord whisper, "PUT ALL YOUR EGGS IN ONE BASKET."

I received this revelation on March 27, 1987. God showed me five eggs that He had given to me which represent five talents that He had placed in my life. He said that the church is the basket. From that moment through today, I have found that my life and passion must be in the church.

A good disciple needs to be passionate about the purpose of God. Part of the way that we can discern God's will for our life is to identify what you are passionate about. Some of us are passionate about everything from food to sports teams, to family, to the church. It's more difficult to discern His will by using the passion principle.

Disciples have their will crossed when somebody says no.

A disciple needs to be teachable, loyal, humble, submissive, persistent, and trustworthy. The problem for many “wannabe disciples” is that they are proud know-it-alls with a little bit of scripture and an oversized ego.

Unteachable disciples run as soon as their will is crossed. Disciples have their will crossed when somebody says no. True disciples do not pout or shout when things don’t go according to their plan. They know how to keep rank, and hold their peace. Most importantly, a true disciple loves God with His whole heart, soul and mind.

Good disciples have a grateful heart. They are flexible. When God shuts one door, they have learned to wait for the Lord to open the next door. The chronology of discipleship goes through four stages – forming, storming, norming and performing. The forming stage is the honeymoon phase. You are born again and everything is perfect. You are in love. God is perfect and the devil is non-existent.

But the honeymoon comes to an end when we find Christians are still people. A new believer’s honeymoon ends when he or she recognize that leaders are not perfect, brothers and sisters still sin, and Christianity means struggle and endurance. Every storm ends. You can wait it out. Don’t panic in the midst of the storm.

Norming comes when the storm blows over. Gone are the questions, the accusations, and the temper tantrums as we submit to His will. We confess with our brother Job, “The Lord gives and the Lord takes away, blessed be the name of the Lord.” It is a time to grow up and put away childishness.

Performing happens when we refocus on His plan that we serve others. This is our time to be a drink offering to those around us. It is a time to grow fruit on our little fruit tree and give it away. If you have love on your tree, give it away.

My favorite book on discipleship is *Connecting*, written by Paul D. Stanley and J. Robert Clinton. They define mentoring as a "relational experience in which one person empowers another by sharing God-given resources." They believe that an actual transfer between mentor and mentoree takes place which they call "empowerment."

Peter imparted healing as he fastened his eyes on the beggar outside of the temple door and said, "I don't have any silver and gold but such as I have I give to you. Rise up and walk." This is a wonderful example of instant impartation. The transfer from mentor to mentoree is usually much slower and less dramatic but with the same result. The mentor is imparting to his disciple the substance of his life and telling the disciple to "rise up and walk."

We all need people who will speak into our lives.

A key to receiving the blessing that God wants to give us begins with accountability. We all need people who will speak into our lives. Positioning for blessing is both vertical and horizontal. We must be vertically connected to the Lord and horizontally connected to people.

Nobody has a monopoly on truth. This key to blessing is about flexibility and teachability. Find your Paul. Find your Timothy. Get ready for your blessing.

13

Taking What is Yours

Position for Blessing - Be Aggressive

WHEN I WAS A YOUNG BOY, I used to play marbles and other games with my brother Don who was two years younger. We found that one thing was certain – when the game was over, I would have all his marbles.

Losing was not an option for me. My brother and I look back on that time and laugh. It was the early manifestation of a philosophy of life. It was important for me to win even if I did not need the marbles (usually I just gave them back to him so that I could win them again).

The Bible says that with "violence the Kingdom of Heaven is taken" (Matt 11:12). Different modern translations and paraphrases interpret this Scripture very differently because the concept of aggression that can be called violence is offensive. But both the New and Old King James Versions say the violent take it.

There are many ways to acquire something: earn it, buy it, inherit it or steal it. Adam and Eve inherited the Garden of Eden and then allowed it to be stolen from them by disobeying the word of God.

Several years ago one of our cars was stolen from in front of our house. The passive man might have said it's okay. The super- spiritual would quote Job, "The Lord gives and the Lord takes away."

But most of us would feel violated, call the police and go looking for our car. We called the police and were rewarded with the return of the little black Honda when the police arrested a young man driving our car.

If you are going to possess the blessing God wants to give, you must practice holy aggression. Even when God has given you His wisdom and direction, it still requires action on your part. In this chapter we will talk about taking what is yours.

I am reminded of a mythical story about a man who lived a long time ago. Because of a crime he committed, the king ordered the man to be beheaded. As the man was being led from the presence of the king, he hollered out to the king, "If you will spare my life, I will teach your horse to fly!" The King's attention was arrested by the man's proclamation so he told the guards to stop.

"Are you lying? Can you really teach my horse to fly?" asked the King.

"Yes. If you will give me a year, I can teach your horse to fly," said the man.

"Alright, I will give you a year to teach my horse to fly. If you are successful in teaching my horse to fly, I will commute your sentence. But if you fail, I will surely behead you," admonished the King. Later a friend of the newly released man asked him about the promise.

"How can you make such a foolish promise? Everybody knows that horses can't fly," said the friend.

"The way I see it three things can happen in the next year: the king could die; I could die; or the horse could fly," said the man who just avoided being executed.

When the thief comes, he does not make an appointment.

This story always brings a smile to my heart as I see a man that refused to quit. He used what he had to stay alive. His greatest asset was his imagination and his willingness to take risks. He was not worried about what people thought about him or even if his promise to the King could be fulfilled. He was doing what he could to stay alive. He understood that life is better than death.

Satan is a thief who has come to kill, steal and destroy (Jn 10:10). When the thief comes, he does not make an appointment. He comes when you least expect it or when you are busy with other things. Satan wants you and your stuff. He did his best to recruit Jesus in the wilderness (Matt 4).

Passive Christians are immobilized by fear, doubt and double mindedness. God promises us that if we submit to God and resist the devil, the devil will flee from us. Even though Satan might have lost the greatest battle for your soul when you were born again, he will not give up.

Satan comes to steal your sobriety, sanity, family, friends, finances, reputation, health, ambition or dream. You name it and Satan will try to steal it. If it has value, expect the thief to try to break in and steal it.

The Lord does not want us to become namby-pamby Christians, wringing our hands. The Lord says MAN UP and move on. Quit looking back, it is time to go forward. God wants you to take back what has been stolen from you. God has given us the power to withstand evil.

Withstand comes from the Greek word "antihistemi." "Anti" means against and "histemi" means to cause to stand. We buy small bottles of "antihistemi" to unplug our nasal passages. But even more important is the need to withstand Satan's fiery darts, deceptions, distractions and derailments.

After we withstand, we need to stand (Eph 6:13-14) and fight. Many years ago I was trying to visit with a Christian friend who kept whispering. I asked him why he was whispering. He told me that the devil could not hear when he whispered and he did not want the devil to hear his plans. This man thought he could avoid conflict by whispering. He forgot that "greater is he that is in you than he that is in this world."

Martin Luther King, Jr. shared his own dream of a special world in his famous speech "I Have a Dream." Satan stole his dream through an assassin's bullet. The devil is the ultimate

Joseph, one of the sons of Jacob, dreamed of honor and success. Joseph owned his dream. He identified with it even though his father was uncertain and his brothers were hostile. Joseph became so identified with his dream that his brothers referred to him as "the dreamer."

Every dream will be tested. Joseph's dream was tested by rejection, slavery, false accusation, imprisonment and being forgotten. Joseph knew where dreams came from and ultimately was released by Pharaoh when he interpreted Pharaoh's dreams.

Joseph is a great example to those of us who dream of His blessing. Joseph found favor with his father, his master, the prison warden and Pharaoh. He passed the test and defeated the dream stealer. God does not want us to be ignorant of Satan's devices. The devil has many tactics and strategies to utilize in his attempt to steal your dream.

Perhaps, the greatest strategy utilized by the devil is unforgiveness. The devil will whisper in you ear that you have been hurt and that you have a right to be bitter. The devil works on our lack of character or immaturity. Wisdom says you will be ruled by the rudder or the rocks. Immature people spend much of their life on the rocks.

Every dream will be tested.

The devil loves the loud and the proud. He knows that loud, proud, stubborn people are rigid, inflexible and unteachable. Pride and stubbornness are two sides of the same coin – the self coin. Satan wants self-centered, immature believers who are inflexible and ungrateful grudge bearers. The devil feeds your fear and starves your faith.

A fictitious story is told about Satan having a big garage sale to get rid of the junk that he had acquired over a long period of time. He had one strange item off to the side marked "not for sale." When asked what the item was, Satan proudly said that it was his best tool. The questioner was still not satisfied and persisted in asking, "What does it do?" Satan said, "When all else fails, I use this tool. I call this tool discouragement."

The dream stealer will do whatever it takes to steal your dream. Faith comes from hearing the Word of God. When God has given you a dream, you will have to fight for it. Don't expect something to happen just because you have dreamed it. "If it was easy, everybody would do it." Don't allow the devil to immobilize you through double mindedness. Faith without works is dead. DIN - do it now.

God has called each of us to be a Somebody.

Bruce Wilkinson has such an ability to articulate, interpret and challenge people to move in God's grace. In *The Dream Giver*, Wilkinson shares a powerful parable about a young man named Ordinary who was a Nobody who lived in a land called Familiar. Ordinary received a big dream from the Dream Giver that he could be a Somebody.

Ordinary's big dream was tested by his friend's negative response and present responsibilities (job, bills, etc.). Ordinary also had to deal with the passing of time and internal doubt. But God confirmed the big dream when Ordinary talked to his father. Ordinary's father shared that he too once had a Big Dream but failed to act on it.

Ordinary needed to leave his Comfort Zone and pass through an invisible Wall of Fear. When Ordinary reached the border and was about to cross over, he was confronted by border bullies who tried to stop him. Champion stepped up and helped Ordinary cross over.

I know that my synopsis of this parable does not do it justice. Buy the book and read it, as God has called each of us to be a Somebody. If we choose to be a Nobody and stay in the land of Familiar, we will never experience all that God has for us.

God is so good about providing Champions to help us during our moments of discouragement. God provided Barnabas to encourage Paul in his walk with the Lord. For us to become the people God has called us to be, we need to find the encouragers. The devil will always be there with his small army of naysayers telling us that it will never happen.

Read the Word until it begins to read you.

When we cannot find a Barnabas, we need to encourage ourselves in the Lord. The ABC's of encouragement are adjust your attitude, be focused on God and confess truth. An airplane needs to fly at the right altitude in order to avoid crashing into wires and other obstacles. Your attitude and your altitude are connected.

Be focused on God's eternal perspective and plan. Fill yourself with the Word of God. Read the Word until it begins to read you. Pray, meditate and worship the one true God. Confess truth, not circumstances. God is faithful even when we are not.

He says that we can do all things and that all things work together for good to those who love Him. Psalm 17:15 says it best. "As for me, I will see your face in righteousness, I shall be satisfied when I awake in your likeness."

God wants to stretch our faith like a rubber band. Rubber bands were created to be stretched. Without stretching, the rubber bands are weak and worthless. Human beings are just like rubber bands created by God to be stretched.

God wants to expand our boundaries through stretching. We need to pray like Jabez and ask God to stretch our boundaries. We will not fulfill our purpose without some stretching. God created us to have relationship with Him. To accomplish this purpose of walking with an invisible God, we must be stretched into the realm of faith.

Many of God's people were stretched in their walk with God. Abraham was stretched when he left his country and again when he offered Isaac on the altar. Isaac was stretched to submit to his crazy father's knife. David was stretched to kill Goliath and not to kill Saul. Esther was stretched to approach the King when she was not called by him.

Peter was stretched to take the gospel to the gentiles. Barnabas was stretched to embrace Paul whose reputation for killing Christians was well known. The greatest stretch of all was Jesus leaving His Father to become a human being.

God wants to expand our boundaries through stretching.

"How you deal with stress will determine the level of your success," I told my son when he started his own law practice.

"I feel so much stress from taking care of clients, paying bills and making all the decisions that I need to make concerning office space, associates, and other stuff," said Dugan.

"If it was easy, everybody would do it."

"Amen to that."

"God is stretching you for His purpose. There is no fulfilling of our destiny without going through an excruciating time of stretching," I shared.

"But how do you know if it is God doing the stretching?" he asked.

"Many Christians have it all wrong as they think if something is easy and fast that it is God. I have found the opposite is true. God takes us to the Promised Land after we have wandered in the wilderness."

"How you deal with stress will determine the level of your success."

I continued, "God uses obstacles and circumstances to build our strength and reveal His power. I pray that it will be quick and easy but prepare myself to endure. When I first came to Christ, I thought it was a sprint. After running as hard as I could for as long as I could, I learned that life in Christ is really an endurance race full of obstacles and surprises."

Sometimes God puts victory in our hands and in our mouths. Samson took a jawbone and killed a thousand enemies (Judg 17:14-17). The widow took empty jars, and in obedience to the prophet, filled them with oil (2 Kings 4:1-7). God wants to stretch our faith.

We overcome by the blood of the Lamb and the word of our testimony. Our mouths can bring victory or destruction. What's in your hand? What's in your mouth?

When Jesus died on the cross, He changed everything. We no longer needed to ask a Levitical priest to pray or offer sacrifices for us. We are a nation of priests. If you are born again, you are a minister of the gospel of Jesus Christ. God wants to speak to you and through you.

In 2 Chronicles 25, God's people were afraid of being conquered by the enemy so they hired a group of mercenaries to fight for them. God told them to forget the mercenaries and trust Him alone for their deliverance.

If you are born again, you are a minister of the gospel of Jesus Christ.

God doesn't want you to recruit others to do what you are called to do. He wants you to trust Him more than parents, pastors or friends. Your family and friends can pray you through the rough spots in life. God rebuked the Israelites for trusting man instead of Him. The victory is in your hand and in your mouth.

God wants you to have an attitude of faith. God wants you to have GODITUDE. We have "goditude" when we realize God loves us and wants to bless us. We put 100% of our faith in Him. The kingdom is ours for the taking. People with "goditude" are not arrogant but focused and determined. They are not standing around waiting for somebody else to fight their battles. We get our attitude from God. We believe His Word and act on it accordingly. My son-in-law, Ryan Murray, calls this "Godfidence."

Trouble is our opportunity to go to another level of faith and maturity. Jesus did not promise us a pain-free, problem-free life. The Word says, "If need be these trials will come upon us." Trouble is a teacher. When the lesson is over, we will be graded on how we did during the middle of the trouble.

Satan stole three things from Adam and Eve: their unbroken fellowship with their Father-Creator; the pure joy of being naked and not ashamed; and legal title to planet earth. Jesus came to destroy the works of the devil and take back all that was stolen. Jesus emptied Himself of all His God-attributes in order to invade our world.

In order to identify completely with us, He became one of us. By dying and rising again, Jesus destroyed the work of the devil. He took back legal title for planet earth, restored fellowship with the Father-Creator and the joy of living without shame.

Trouble trains us by revealing what is in our hearts, purifying and purging us from carnality, and preparing us for what is next. Trouble works for us when we humble ourselves, repent and search for God. Trouble works against us when we get angry and try to solve the problems through our own efforts. When you have a self-view of circumstances, you miss out on God's perspective and purpose.

Trouble is a part of all of our lives, as the rain falls on the just and the unjust. Job said, "I am not at ease nor am I quiet, I have no rest for trouble comes" (Job 3:26). Job went on to say that man is born of a woman and has a few days of trouble. David was also no stranger to trouble. David knew that "in time of trouble, God will hide us in His tabernacle" (Ps 27:4-5).

Trouble is a part of all of our lives.

Jesus told us to be prepared for trouble (Jn 16:33). Tribulations come and go just like the weather. Troubles are trials that demand we stay strong.

Jesus told Martha that only one thing was needful and Mary chose that. We need to choose eternity over now, life over death, blessing over cursing and treasure over trouble. How you handle trouble will determine your destiny. There is no immunization from trouble. Everybody needs to prepare their hearts and go through it. His blessing is just on the other side of the trouble.

To get the blessing, we need to take it!

Too many of us live a simple, superficial, hedonistic form of Christianity. We believe that we are entitled to live without pressures and problems. But the reality is that there is no such thing.

God wants to bless and we want the blessing. We need to take it in the midst of fears and doubts. We need to persevere in faith when trials test us. To get the blessing, we need to take it back from the devil or the circumstance holding onto it.

14

Confess and Possess

Position for Blessing - Confess Truth

HAVE YOU EVER WONDERED why some people have all the luck? Does God love one person more than another person? Or, are there some secret principles for success? I believe that there are secrets to success. These secrets are hidden from the lazy, the proud and the unbeliever.

"It is the glory of God to conceal a matter but the glory of kings to search out a matter" (Prov 25:2). When Jesus spoke the parable of the sower, He said that it was given to His disciples to know the mysteries of the Kingdom.

During the 1970s a controversial teaching became prominent throughout Christianity. It was derogatorily referred to as "blab it, grab it" or "name it, claim it." The teaching found its roots within the teaching of faith.

The core of this teaching is that we have a good and loving God who wants to give His children every good and perfect gift. We need to confess and possess the blessing of the Lord. Many Christians believed this teaching to be heresy because it shifted the focus from the cross to worldly possessions.

"As a man thinks in his heart so is he," proclaims the book of Proverbs. Likewise, "A man is snared by the words of his mouth." When God created the world and everything in it, He simply opened His mouth and spoke. God said, "Let there be light," and there was light. God said, "Let there be firmament," and there was substance.

God said, "Let the waters be gathered," and the oceans were formed. God said, "Let the earth bring forth grass," and there was grass. God said, "Let the earth bring forth the living creature according to its kind," and there were animals. And then God said, "Let us make man in Our image, according to Our likeness," and there was Adam.

You have to speak your faith.

God's greatest creation was made in His image and likeness. Man was made to have dominion, to be fruitful and multiply. This book is an attempt to uncover secrets that lead to blessing. Jesus said, "The works that I do shall you do also and greater works for I go to the Father."

Jesus' ministry was spent just like the Father. He created wine from water, multiplied fish and loaves, and healed by opening His mouth and speaking. "See it, say it" was the God-created method used first by the Father and then by the Son.

Jesus teaches us to take dominion when He cursed the fig tree for its failure to produce fruit (Mk 11). The secret begins with having faith in God. "Whoever says to this mountain be removed and not doubt in his heart shall have what he says," Jesus instructed His disciples. You have to speak your faith. The unspoken prayer requests will not be answered no matter how religiously righteous they might appear.

Jesus tells us to speak our faith against any obstacle that is in our way. Speak out against poverty, joblessness, divorce, addiction and any other problem that stands in your way of being blessed. An obstacle is something too big to go around, too big to go over or too big to tunnel through. You need to tell your problems where to go. I love offending the religious when I tell the devil to go to HELL. I'm just telling the devil to go home.

Jesus says, "Don't doubt in your heart." Believe what you say. I remember years ago pointing at a boat marina and telling about sixty people on a boat that I intended to own that property.

"Do you see that marina?" I asked.

After they all looked, I said, "I intend to own that property. I have no money and no deal but I have faith and I have God."

Christians are called to see with ears an invisible God.

Faith is the substance of things not seen. Jesus says, "Only believe." Later, I did have a contract for the purchase of the boat marina where we operated our law firm, travel agency, marina, and two restaurants. "You will have whatever you say," said Jesus.

The secret of confession and possession is believing and trusting in God who is the author and finisher of our faith. The early disciples understood this and asked Jesus to increase their faith (Luke 17:1-6). "If you have faith as much as a mustard seed," you can move mountains. More powerful than nuclear power is the power of faith.

Christians are called to see with ears an invisible God (Rom 10:17). Blind men see through their ears. Their ears become their eyes and allow them to make decisions as to where they are, who they are talking to, etc. People of faith are no different than a blind man. We see with our spiritual ears.

To practice the principle of confession/possession you have to make a paradigm shift from cleverness and manipulation, from self-help to God-help and from self-reliance to God-reliance. What do you see? Do you see the future and hope that God has for you – a house, a car, a relationship? Do you see the American dream?

Our faith is not in our education, our cleverness, our luckiness, or ourselves but in His love and sufficiency.

A good confession is more than something a Catholic says to the priest in a confessional. It is confessing to the world that Jesus is the only way, the only truth and the only life. Our lips and lives need to be in sync if we want to reap the benefits of being children of God.

Into the genre of reality television shows (*American Idol, Biggest Loser, Survivor,* etc.) came a show called *The Moment of Truth.* The contestants are administered a detailed polygraph examination prior to appearing on the show. They have family and friends sitting off to the side while they are asked a series of potentially embarrassing questions that they will be tempted to lie about.

The goal is to answer truthfully and ultimately receive the grand prize of $500,000. They are asked about sex, money, stealing, lying, relationships and other embarrassing issues. When the question is asked, it is the moment of truth. Will they lie or tell the truth?

Christianity is the ultimate moment of truth. What do we do with Jesus who said that He was truth? This is the question that Pontius Pilate wrestled with when he met Jesus. Pilate asked, "What is truth?" What you do with the ultimate moment of truth determines your eternal destiny.

God tells us that there will be a new heaven and a new earth (Rev 21:1-8) where the lion lays down with the lamb. There will be no more lying, dying or crying. We will dance on streets of gold as we worship the one true God. That is the good news for those who are born again.

But not everybody will receive Jesus as Lord and Savior. Revelation tells us that there are many who will not make it to Heaven but will spend eternity in the Lake of Fire. This list includes the cowardly (or fearful), the unbelieving, the abominable, murderers, sexually immoral people, sorcerers, idolaters, and ALL LIARS. It is simple – you lie, you die.

Christianity is the ultimate moment of truth.

The biggest lie ever told was spoken by the father of lies when he told Adam and Eve, "You shall not die" (Gen 3:4). Satan's very nature is to lie. He is known as a liar and deceiver. The Bible says that you are a liar if you deny Christ (1 Jn 2:22) or if you say that you love Christ but hate your brother. (1 Jn 4:20)

"Thou shalt not bear false witness against your neighbor" is one of the Ten Commandments. Perjury is a crime in every society. Proverbs says, "It is better to be poor than a liar" (Prov 19:22).

God wants us to be men and women of integrity. It is an abomination to lie. Our word is our bond. Some of us have the "Peter Problem" which is recorded in all four Gospels. Jesus prophesied Peter's lie when he told Peter, "Before the rooster crows, you will deny me three times."

The rooster crowed after Peter lied three times. Many of us have been dulled into deafness so that we no longer hear the rooster crowing when we lie.

Remember the story about the wooden puppet that was brought to life by fairy dust. Every time Pinocchio lied, his nose grew longer. When the puppet wanted to know how the fairy knew that he was lying, the fairy said something profound:

> "Lies, my boy, are recognized at once, because they are of only two kinds. Some have short legs and others have long noses. Yours are the kind with long noses."

Many years ago I had a deacon in my church that was having marital problems. His wife was convinced that he was having an affair, so I went and asked him if it was true.

"Tom (not his real name), your wife has told me that you are having an affair. Is it true?" I asked him.

He looked me in the eye and said, "It's not true. My wife is paranoid. She is imagining this."

Later I was told by his paramour (who was not part of the church) that they were having an affair. I immediately went to the deacon, confronted him and asked him why he lied.

"I couldn't tell you the truth. You would have kicked me out of the church." He justified his lie on the basis that I would tell his wife and boot him out of the church. The Bible says that our hidden sins shall find us out.

There is a story about a father who took his daughter with him as he went out to steal from the neighbor's field. The father told the daughter, "Call out if anyone sees me."

As the father stole from the first field, the daughter called, "Father, someone sees you." She did the same on the second, third and final field. The father angrily asked his daughter, "Why in the world do you keep saying someone sees me? I've looked everywhere and I didn't see anyone." The little girl looked at her father and said, "Father, Someone sees you from above."

There is no place to hide from the truth. We need to commit ourselves to be truth tellers. *The Moment of Truth* is more than a game – it is life. Peter repented for his lying and so should we. If we mess up, we fess up. I don't want my life to be spent hearing the "rooster crowing."

God says, "Out of the same mouth proceed blessing and cursing" (Jas 3:10). Jesus said that it was not what goes into our mouths that defile us but what comes out (Matt 15:11). God is not the author of confusion. He does not speak with a "forked tongue." My tongue is the rudder that directs my life the same way that a rudder directs a ship.

I don't want my life to be spent hearing the "rooster crowing."

The tongue can be an

instrument of destruction. It can cut and kill like a sword or be a blunt instrument like a hammer. It can be a slimy, slithering snake biting and devouring. There is a particular snake that emits a slimy fluid on the mouse that it intends to eat. Many times people flatter or "slime" us just before they make their run at swallowing us. The tongue is oftentimes an instrument of betrayal and deception of family and friends.

It does not have to be like this. The tongue can do so much more than lie, curse and deceive. God wants us to use our tongues to praise Him. A fountain does not bring forth both bitter and sweet water.

God wants His children to have a HAPPY TONGUE. David said that he had a happy tongue because the "Lord is always before my face" (Acts 2:25-28). David had so many things that made his tongue happy: God was on his right hand; his body was resting in hope; God would not leave him in the grave nor allow him to be corrupted. God made known the ways of life. Acts 2:25-28 says it especially well in The Message Version:

> "I saw God before me for all time. Nothing can shake me; He's right by my side. I'm glad from the inside out, ecstatic; I've pitched my tent in the land of hope. I know You'll never dump me in the land of Hades; I'll never even smell the stench of death. You've got my feet on the life-path, with Your face shining sun-joy all around."

People with happy tongues are focused, believing and confident in His grace and mercy. Happy tongues lead to happy faces. Sad-sacks are self-focused and unbelieving. "Glad-sacks" are God-focused, believing and full of a good confession about God and circumstances. What kind of a sack are you?

God wants our tongues to be trees of life (Prov 15:3). One of the first things that doctors do when we go for a physical is have us open our mouth so that they can check our tongue.

It's the same in the spirit world. God says that "out of the mouth proceed the thoughts and intents of the heart." A lying tongue is sick. A deceptive tongue is diseased. And a cancerous tongue is infectious.

What kind of a sack are you?

When a tree tongue is dead, it's good for nothing but firewood. If the tree appears to be sick, we call the tree surgeon to come examine and treat the tree.

Several years ago, I called Sterling, the tree surgeon, to come and examine three trees. The leaves and needles on the trees had turned brown. Our tree surgeon (aka gardener) told us that the trees were dead and needed to be cut down. It was too late to save the trees through water or fertilizer.

Sterling, the master gardener said,

> "Brown leaves don't turn green. Be sure you pull off all the brown and yellow leaves. BROWN LEAVES NEVER TURN GREEN. Dead limbs don't produce fruit. Spent blooms need to be picked from the plant. Excess growth needs to be severely pruned. It's a lot of work, and for a while the plants may look worse for all the effort. Eventually new growth, new buds, new flowers and fruit will come –

provided the basic plant is still alive at the root level."

As a pastor, every day I help people identify leaves and limbs that have to go. Dead leaves and limbs are old habits, addictions, thought patterns and beliefs (conscious or unconscious) that need to be removed. Jesus is the ultimate tree surgeon. He says, "If your eye causes you to sin pluck it out. If your hand causes you to sin, cut it off."

All of life involves the two original trees found in the Garden of Eden – the tree of knowledge of good and evil represents man and the tree of life represents God. Man was created to have fellowship with God. Even as God is triune, so is man. Man is a spirit made in the image and likeness of God who has a soul (mind, will and emotions) that lives in a body.

Every day I help people identify leaves and limbs that have to go.

Too many Christians live their lives eating at the tree of knowledge, believing all of life can be understood with the intellect. Many who eat at this tree have concluded that there is no God, man has evolved from a fish (or is it an ape?) and this is all there is.

An atheist who ate his full from the tree of knowledge brought a lawsuit alleging discrimination since Christian holidays like Christmas and Easter were celebrated but there was no holiday for the atheist.

The judge listened to all the legal arguments and then banged his gavel and dismissed the case. The judge concluded that the atheist's argument was without foundation as the atheists already had an annual holiday. The lawyer for the atheist quickly jumped to his feet.

"I don't understand Your Honor. When is the special holiday for atheists?" asked the lawyer.

"Why it's every year on April 1," said the judge.

"Forgive me your Honor, but I don't understand how you can conclude that April 1 is a holiday to commemorate atheism. Would you please explain?" implored the attorney.

"Yes. I would be glad to. It's really quite simple. The Bible says, 'The fool says in his heart there is no God.' April 1 is known as All Fools Day," concluded the judge.

Your tongue is your personal tree of life. Are you producing green leaves, healthy limbs and fruit that will last? If not, let the master gardener trim away dead habits and addictions. Let the master gardener remove the dead leaves and limbs. You are called to be a tree of righteousness. Your tongue tells the world what you really believe.

The world is broken down into two major groups – the haves and the have-nots. The former Third World is now referred to as the Two-Thirds world as a more accurate numerical depiction of those that have not. Those with money and goods are the haves while those without money and goods are the have-nots.

Your tongue is your personal tree of life.

God's plan has always been to take His people from the land of "not enough" (Egypt) through the land of "just enough" (the wilderness) to the land of "more than enough" (the Promised Land). The Promised Land is a land of milk and honey.

You are either blessed or unblessed. Our confession sets the table of blessing by speaking the word of God into our circumstances. We do not have to lie to God or to ourselves but we do need to learn how to confess God's promises if we intend to be blessed.

God wants to bring the "have-nots" into the Promised Land. This book is setting out some of the secret or forgotten principles related to getting into and staying in the Promised Land. God says, "You have not because you ask not" (Jas 4:3). Our confession is instrumental to our receiving His blessing.

God wants to send us blessing. His eye is looking for somebody to bless and His ear is open to those who call on His name. By confessing truth and aligning ourselves with truth, we position ourselves for the blessing that comes from God.

15

Disciplined and Blessed

Position for Blessing - Be Disciplined

GOD WILL LEAD YOU (AND BLESS YOU) the easiest way you let Him. God's heart is to love and bless His children. His eye is looking for somebody to bless. After over forty years of watching God bless some and not others, I have discovered some secrets to receiving the blessing.

Although the rain falls on the just and the unjust, God blesses the diligent and the disciplined even more. The world says, "The early bird gets the worm." God says, "It's not fitting to honor a fool."

There are many spiritual disciplines that help position you to receive God's blessing. The most important is to become a self- feeding Christian. God says, "Man shall not live by bread alone but by every Word that proceeds out of the mouth of God" (Matt 4:4). The Bible is the literal, verbal expression of the will and plan of God.

It does not contain the Word of God. The Bible is the "logos" of God while Jesus is the "Rhema" (i.e. personal revelation) of God. We don't worship the logos of God but are changed, challenged and sanctified by its truth. It shapes our values, opinions, thoughts and emotions. It picks our friends and tells us right from wrong.

Adam and Eve were the original members of the Fellowship of Line-Crossers.

Adam and Eve received the simple Word of God. He told them to enjoy themselves but not to eat the fruit from the tree of knowledge of good and evil. Many of us are just like Adam and Eve – the one thing we are told not to do becomes the primary focus of our interest.

"You and I are just alike," I said as I looked out on my congregation of drug addicts, prostitutes and criminals.

"We have seen a line in the sand and been told not to step over the line. Most of us get our feet right up to the line and dangle our toes over it, debating the consequences of the warning. Everything within us wants to step over the line and see what happens."

Adam and Eve were the original members of the Fellowship of Line-Crossers. They were probably standing next to the one tree that they were told to stay away from when Satan came with his lies and deception. This was a catastrophic decision for all of mankind as Adam and Eve exchanged the Word of God for the law of conscience.

Their conscience told them they were naked and needed to cover up. Their conscience felt guilty for their disobedience so they tried to hide from the voice of God. Plan A was to simply walk in the presence of God and do what He said. Instead man decided that he had a better idea.

We need to do what the Word of God says even if we have no little policeman blowing the whistle (aka conscience). By prolonged and repeated sin, some of us have lost the ability to feel guilt. The liar lies so much that he (or she) no longer feels anything when he tells another lie. So is it with the thief, the adulterer, the gossip, the drunk and every other person who habitually sins for a long enough period of time.

From the time I first came to Christ, I determined to read the Bible in its entirety each year. For the first years of our marriage, my wife and I selected a different translation each year and read it together.

In 1980 I was coordinating a visit from Jerry Falwell and the Moral Majority to Helena, Montana. It was part of his plan to visit all fifty state capitals. The Liberty University singers arrived a day early to get set up for a special performance in the capital city. As I was visiting with the Liberty University bus driver, he pointed at one of the young men and told me a story that challenged me to rethink my commitment to read the Bible once a year.

"Do you see that young man over there?" asked the bus driver as he pointed at an ordinary looking young man.

"Yeah, I see him," I said.

"Do you mind if I tell you a story?" asked the driver.

"No. I am all ears. Tell me a story," I said, sensing that I was about to hear something really special.

"The young man is preparing himself to go to Russia as a student. In preparation for his trip, he is doing two things – learning Russian and reading the Bible from Genesis to Revelation every month," explained the driver.

By His grace, I surprised myself by reading the Bible in its entirety in 30 days.

"What? Did you say that he's reading the entire Bible every month?"

"Yes. You heard right. He knows that when he goes to Russia to study, he will not be able to bring a Bible, so he is filling himself with the Word. His purpose is to win his roommate and as many of his classmates and associates as he can for Christ during his time in Russia," explained the bus driver.

My mind was arrested by the thought of reading the entire Bible in a month. I was not sure if I was willing to sacrifice enough to do that. But I wanted to try.

I didn't tell anybody but my wife what I was trying to do as I thought that it was highly likely that I would not get through the Word in that period of time. I remember sitting at the kitchen table at midnight reading with tired, bloodshot eyes because the day had been too busy and I had not found the time to read for three hours.

I took the Bible with me everywhere. It went with me to the bathroom. It rode with me in the car for five or ten minutes of reading between appointments.

By His grace, I surprised myself (and probably my wife too) by reading the Bible in its entirety in 30 days. I thought it might have been a fluke, so I did it a second month. Upon successfully completing the second month, I told the church what I had done. About twenty-six people joined me for month three as we successfully read the entire Bible in a month.

This story is not about me being a great man of God. It's about bringing the discipline of reading the Word of God into your home and life. How can you do what God wants if you do not know what He thinks? How can you have the mind of Christ when you have never taken the time to feed your spirit with His Word?

When we first come to Christ we read the Word over and over until it becomes ingrained in our spirit. At some point, we have so much of the Word within us that THE WORD READS US. It reads our motivations and tells us when we are play acting and when we are real.

The first book that I attempted to write was called *Babies Can't Eat T-Bones*. I was trying to make the point that sometimes our expectations were too high and our food too complex for the toothless babies who were still in their diapers.

The book was an attempt to teach people how to feed themselves. The Bible says that the borrower is servant to the lender. If you are always borrowing revelation and insight from other Christians, you are always going to be a baby. You will be an echo and not a voice. God says dig your own well (or cistern).

We need to be like the cow chewing its cud when we come to meditating on the Word of God. A cow swallows, regurgitates and chews some more before digesting the food provided. This is a good image of mediation for believers who want to digest the Word of God.

May my meditation be sweet, writes the Psalmist (Ps 104:34). Instead, many of us meditate on our problems, pressures, hurts and fears. God says if there is something good, we should meditate or think on that. We need to gGet our mind out of the gutter and into the Word.

In 1973 when I first got out of law school, I bought a wire-haired Griffon and named her Faith. My wife Cathy and I thought that naming the dog Faith would cause us to be built up whenever we called her.

The opposite actually occurred as we began to think of faith as our dog rather than as believing in the invisible God of the universe. Well, one day our dog Faith was left in the car by herself. I think she must have been hungry for the Word of God as she ate the first thirty-two chapters of the book of Genesis.

Later I took the Bible devoured by Faith and stood before my congregation asking for a volunteer to step forward and eat the Word of God. I did not tell them the story of my dog but of Jeremiah, Ezekiel, John and Jesus who all ate the Word of God.

I tore a page from the Bible and began to eat it.

One fellow quickly stepped up thinking that I wanted him to merely pretend to eat the Word. I tore a page from the Bible and began to eat it. He quickly took a page and also began to eat it. Of course, there were people repelled by this demonstration but they did get the idea. The Word of God needs to become a part of us.

The Psalmist says, "Thy Word have I hid in my heart that I might not sin against thee." We are to speak it, pray it, hear it, heed it and preach it. Jesus asked His disciples and others, "Have you not read?" (Matt 12:1-5; 19:3-5; and 22:31-33). The Word is what tells us right from wrong, good from evil.

We need to give attendance to reading (1Tim 4:13). We need to study as a workman because God's Word is God's will. It's a light that cleanses and comforts us. Heaven and earth will pass away but God's Word will not.

Another great spiritual discipline is prayer (aka talking to God). God says that His house is a "House of Prayer" (Luke 19:46). Oswald Chambers says, "Prayer is not an exercise, it is the life."

William Carey, the great prayer warrior, said, "Prayer – secret, fervent, believing prayer – lies at the root of all personal godliness."

Most believers feel guilty that they don't pray enough. The Bible says that we are to pray without ceasing. We live in the real world with kid's activities, jobs, meals and all the rest of the stuff that needs to be tended to. With all this stuff, is it realistic to "pray without ceasing?"

"God does nothing but in answer to prayer."

Richard Foster says, "Certain things will happen in history if we pray rightly. We are to change the world by prayer." John Wesley agrees, "God does nothing but in answer to prayer."

The disciples came to Jesus and said, "Teach us to pray" (Luke 11:1). The Bible is full of people who prayed. We have Moses pleading with God, Israel crying out, Hezekiah turning his face to the wall and Hannah crying out in her barrenness.

Daniel and his buddies Shadrach, Meshach and Abednego were serious prayer warriors. Each of these remarkable leaders chose to pray in the face of opposition. Esther prayed, "If I perish, I perish." When Job prayed, "God turned his captivity" (Job 42:10).

In 1998, Cathy and I began hosting foreign students who came to America from all over the world to learn English. One of these students was a practicing Muslim from Saudi Arabia. One of the first questions he asked me was which direction was east. As a faithful Muslim, He was devoted to praying in the direction of Mecca. This young Muslim was more faithful to cry out to his God daily and diligently than most Christians.

Prayer is not meant to be fun. It is work!

The Bible says that Jesus is seated at the right hand of the Father making intercession for you and me. When the disciples prayed, the place was shaken. Prayer needs to be our life.

We can pray on top of the mountain, in the wilderness, standing, kneeling or prostrate. We can pray driving down the highway, in the city or on the seashore. We pray for those who despitefully use us (Luke 6:28). We pray for wisdom, healing, reconciliation and deliverance. If you can think it, you can pray it.

Prayer is not meant to be fun. It is work – the work of the ministry. Pastor Larry Lee taught that prayer is digging holes, setting posts, stringing wire, transmitting and receiving. Most of that is just old fashioned work. It is wonderful when God comes on the line and speaks to us.

The old song says, "I've just heard from Heaven, and it's all right now." God solves problems, lifts burdens, changes hearts and confirms direction in seconds when He speaks to our hearts in a time of prayer.

Richard Foster said, "Prayer is like any other work: we may not feel like working, but once we have been at it for a bit, we begin to feel like working."

There are times when it is wrong to pray. God told Jeremiah, "Don't pray" (Jer 7:16), and he told Joshua, "Quit praying" (Josh 7:10). When prayer is a substitute for doing what God has already told us to do, it's wrong! Joshua was more comfortable lying on his face calling out to God than getting up and dealing with the sin in the camp.

"...prayer changes me and I change things."

Others want to pray to be seen, like the Pharisee standing in the front of the temple. Wanting people to look at you as you pray is a clear sign of superficiality. Others ask God for stuff without any connection to blessing others or the Kingdom of God (Jas 4:2).

Perhaps the best words on prayer come from that giant prayer warrior Oswald Chambers who said:

> "It is not so true that 'prayer changes things' as that prayer changes me and I change things. God has so constituted things that prayer on the basis of Redemption alters the way in which a man looks at things. Prayer is not a question of altering things externally, but of working wonders in a man's disposition."

Another spiritual discipline that demands some attention for those desiring His presence and blessing is fasting. The Bible says that our weapons are mighty to the pulling down of strongholds. Fasting is the forgotten weapon, as we do not want to humble ourselves through depriving the flesh of its supremacy. As a young Catholic boy, I fasted from meat every Friday. During Lent I joined other Catholics in fasting from candy or some other pleasurable food.

In the first week of my new life as a Christian, I was sustained by His presence and His Word as I walked in God's first words to me, "Don't eat!" I devoured the Scriptures, saw visions, prayed and attempted to obey Him in everything He was saying. I did not even know that I was fasting. All I knew was that the Lord said don't eat, and that I was hungry for only one thing – His presence.

Fasting is a time of humbling ourselves before the Lord.

During the seven days of not eating, I learned that I was actually practicing the spiritual discipline of fasting. Jesus said that our power to cast out demons is connected to our commitment to fast and pray (Matt 17:14-21).

James Earl Massey teaches a clear and convincing word on why Christians need to fast. Massey said:

> "Fasting is important in Christian experience because it deepens within the whole self a sense of one's dependence upon the strength of God. Fasting is more than an act of abstinence. It is an affirmative act; it is a way of waiting on God; it is an act of surrender."

Beginning from that time of "don't eat," I spent many days and nights surrendering to God through the discipline of fasting. Some have broadened the concept of fasting to encompass people giving up their cell phones, television shows or nightly glass of gin and tonic. But Alexander Schememann says,

> "Ultimately to fast means only one thing: to be hungry – to go to the limit of human condition which depends entirely on food and, being hungry, to discover that this dependency is not the whole truth about us, that hunger itself is first of all a spiritual state and that it is in its last reality hunger for God."

Again, my initial venture into fasting was a total statement of hunger for God. Fasting is a time of humbling ourselves before the Lord. "More than any other discipline, fasting reveals the things that control us," writes Richard Foster.

Before his own sin was exposed, I heard Pastor Ted Haggard, author of *Primary Purpose,* say that he required all his church leaders to fast three consecutive days each month. Haggard said that he wanted the anger, lust, greed and other flaws to come out during a regular fast rather than through a blow-up, adultery or theft.

Affirming Haggard's teaching on fasting, Richard Foster says in *Celebration of Discipline*,

> "Anger, bitterness, jealousy, strife, fear – if they are within us - they will surface during fasting. At first we will rationalize that our anger is due to our hunger, then we will realize that we are angry because the spirit of anger is within us."

Fasting re-establishes our right priorities. Jesus was led by the Spirit to the wilderness where He fasted and prayed His way through every test that the devil could throw at him (Matt 4). He found His strength in hearing the voice of the Father and doing His will. Foster goes on to say, "Our human cravings and desires are like rivers that tend to overflow their banks; fasting helps keep them in their proper channels."

Fasting is a privilege more than a command. John Wesley refused to ordain anybody who would not fast two days a week. Jesus says, "When you fast..." (Matt 6:16). He told those who asked why His own disciples did not fast, "When the bridegroom is gone then they will fast" (Matt 9:15).

If our hands are full, they are full of the things we are addicted to.

The early disciples ministered unto the Lord and fasted. They knew that they needed to focus on His strength and sufficiency through humbling their souls.

God speaks and works when we humble ourselves through fasting. Gerald May argues that fasting helps us break unwanted, life-destroying addictions. In his book, *Addiction and Grace: Love and Spirituality in the Healing of Addictions,* he says:

> "St. Augustine once said that God is always trying to give good things to us, but our hands are too full to receive them. If our hands are full, they are full of the things we are addicted to. And not only our hands, but also our hearts, minds and attention are clogged with addiction. Our addictions fill up the spaces within us, spaces where God might flow...The

> spiritual significance of addiction is not just that we lose freedom through attachment to things...but that we try to fulfill our longing for God through objects of attachment."

Through my forty plus years of serving the Lord there have been numerous fasts. As I get older, the length of the fast has become shorter (and I am ashamed to admit the length between fasts longer). My stomach has grown larger over time and my appetite for God is satisfied in less painful disciplines.

The first year of my Christian life was spent with more days fasting than eating. Food was irrelevant. I wanted Him more than anything else. I was attending law school at the time and found myself repeatedly praying that God would flunk me out so that I could give myself to carrying a sign that said, "Turn or Burn."

During my first pastorate, I began to fast and pray with a couple of brothers. As days turned into weeks, I sensed that God wanted me to fast for 40 days. My friends dropped out at twenty days but I felt compelled to press through to the end.

I remember that God was so special but no earth-shattering revelations seemed to come to me. At twenty days, I sensed the Lord say to me, "The heart is deceitful and desperately wicked." I told the Lord that I knew that from Jeremiah 17:9. After forty days, I sensed the Lord say, "Your heart is deceitful and desperately wicked."

I am not an advocate of the super-long fast, as God can do in our hearts what needs to be done as we regularly fast a day a week or three days a month. I have had many ten- and fifteen-day fasts, but have found the greatest fruit in denying the cry of the flesh by humbling it on a regular basis.

I felt compelled to fast for forty days one more time as I was searching for the mind of Christ about starting another church in California. Out of this intense time, I sensed God give me quiet confidence to start Open Arms Christian Center. Macrina Wiederkehr said it best when she wrote in *A Tree Full of Angels*,

> "Fasting makes me vulnerable and reminds me of my frailty. It leads me to remember that if I am not fed I will die...Standing before God hungry, I suddenly know who I am. I am the one who is poor, called to be rich in a way that the world does not understand. I am the one who is empty called to be filled with the fullness of God. I am the one who is hungry, called to take all the goodness that can be mine in Christ."

Wiederkehr reminds us that fasting cleanses us as we bare our souls. We go from hunger in the natural to a hunger for justice, goodness and holiness. Fasting might leave you weak and dizzy, with bad breath and a grumbling stomach.

In the Old Testament, everybody fasted including the babies, the animals and the moms with newborn babies.

Foster adds, "In many ways the stomach is like a spoiled child, and a spoiled child does not need indulgence, but needs discipline.

Martin Luther says, "...the flesh was wont to grumble dreadfully.' You must not give in to this grumbling. Ignore the signals, or even tell your spoiled child to calm down and in a brief time the hunger pangs will pass."

Fasting is a spiritual discipline that cannot be ignored. It is no less important than reading the Word or prayer. If you want to receive from the Father all of His blessings, you need to practice more than one of these disciplines.

Another discipline that causes us to come face to face with the Lord is worship. We worship by bowing down, esteeming in reverence.

Foster says "to worship is to experience reality, to touch life. It is to know, to feel, to experience the resurrected Christ in the midst of the gathered community."

Jesus expects us to worship in spirit and truth (Jn 4:19-24). Foster says it correctly when he says, "We have not worshipped the Lord until Spirit touches spirit."

"In many ways the stomach is like a spoiled child..."

Too many of us choose to be Martha Christians - busy serving the Lord and those around us instead of wrapping ourselves around the feet of Jesus. Jesus commended Mary for she chose that which was needful.

Foster points out that "activity is the enemy of adoration." We are to present our bodies a living sacrifice which is our reasonable service. Worship is not about us but about Him who deserves our adoration.

Before he died, missionary Mike Tappan used to challenge the River of Life churches in the Philippines by saying, "It's all about Jesus." Out of this strong emphasis on the reason for every season, a spirit of worship arose. Even though Mike went to be with the Lord about seven years ago, the spirit of worship continues on, for it was firmly embedded into the DNA of the churches that he planted.

Many years ago, I led worship in our Helena church. I found that I could do this effectively with my limited gifting if I placed a strong singer on each side of me. They were tasked with the responsibility of staying on key and remembering the words to the songs. My task was to sense His Spirit and to find the "holy place" where we could be touched.

Through the years I have encouraged people to believe God for healing and miracles during a time of worship. This is a special time when the presence of the Lord is so strong that the impossible becomes possible. God wants to walk among the golden candlesticks (aka His people).

Worship is not about us but about Him who deserves our adoration.

Worship services will either build people up or wear people out. The sole goal of every worship leader is to simply lead the people into the presence of the Lord. It's a time for people to cast their burdens on the Lord. It's a time of refreshment, restoration and recommitment. God wants our whole being to cry, "Holy, holy, holy is the Lord."

By embracing spiritual disciplines we can avoid drifting from the purpose of God. Spiritual disciplines are so necessary to position us for the blessings that God wants to give us. Every true spiritual discipline should bring us into a closer, more intimate relationship with Jesus Christ.

16

Choosing to be a Risk-Taker

Position for Blessing - Take Risks

IT WAS JUST A POLITE QUESTION to get to know one of the guys in the recovery program. When I asked Ricky what he wanted to be, he said, "I want to become a millionaire." Then he asked me if I would help him. I told him that it was never too late but that becoming a millionaire would require work and discipline. Many of us want things - money, recognition or something else. However, we usually get what we work for or have faith for.

My father was a wonderful man who chose the security of a modest government job to take care of his family rather than become the super salesman that he was gifted to be. He provided well for his wife and five children. He sacrificed to send us to college and inspired us to stay and get our degrees.

However, he was damaged by the deprivations of the great depression. He could have done much more but was stopped by his fear of the future.

Even before I came to Christ, I made a decision to live a fearless life. I chose to become a risk taker. The truth is that you and I have the life that we have chosen. You are not merely a victim of poverty or fate. Your life is the result of hundreds of decisions.

In 1973 when I graduated from law school, I was appointed the county attorney for a small, rural county in eastern Montana. It was a part-time position that required me to prosecute crime and advise the Garfield County officials. We lived in Jordan, Montana which was the county seat and the only incorporated town in the county. There were about 500 people in the town and 1,700 in the county.

Even before I came to Christ, I made a decision to live a fearless life.

All the little decisions we began to make during that time in our lives shaped a philosophy of risk taking. We were in Jordan, Montana for a short time when I decided we should buy a 2,400 square foot house that everybody thought was totally overpriced at $16,000.

After contacting the seller who had moved away about a year earlier, I bought the house for $11,000 (assumed his mortgage of $10,300 and executed two promissory notes for $350). I found that if you had the courage to take a risk, you could buy something with no money. Four years later, we sold the house for $40,000. That was a phenomenal profit in such a short time.

Cathy was very upset with how fast and aggressive I was in pursuing and purchasing this three-bedroom home. She thought that I was going to bankrupt us and suggested that I call her dad or mine. I refused to do this. It seemed foolish since my dad did not even own his own house and Cathy's father was not a real estate mogul.

Even though she cried, I was determined to buy the house. God was merciful and brought her parents to visit us at that time. They looked at the house and thought it seemed like a good deal. Her fears disappeared with the approval of her parents. I learned that it takes time for a young bride to trust her husband the way she does her father.

I remember this first house transaction for two reasons – it was such a good deal but it took the faith of a stranger (me) to see it and buy it. The second reason was that Cathy's initial aversion to taking risks was overcome by multiple purchases that worked out for the good. Later, I would buy a property for almost $300,000 without Cathy even looking at it before we were in escrow.

Risk taking is about hearing the Lord's voice and getting out of the boat.

Our time in Jordan, Montana was a time of learning and growing. We learned to depend on the Lord for His wisdom about buying and doing. We bought my law office and the local post office which was part of the same building for $20,000 on an owner-financed contract for deed. Again, God was blessing us when we had no great banking connections or personal savings.

We bought the building occupied by another law firm that drove to Jordan once a week. We bought the land on both sides of us and moved a little old house to Hell Creek State Park located on Fort Peck Reservoir. We bought a twenty-four foot boat, cowboy boots and cars. It was like the Lord allowed us to live a lifetime in four years.

I am challenged by John Ortberg's book *If You Want To Walk on Water, You've Got To Get Out Of The Boat.* Peter was more than impulsive Peter, he was the risk taker that got out of the boat at the voice of Jesus and walked on water.

Risk taking is about hearing the Lord's voice and getting out of the boat. It can be fun to take a chance if you know that nothing bad is going to happen. But in real life, there is always the real possibility that something bad is going to happen.

I have never been too concerned about the "boat sitters" laughing at me...

Cathy and I have learned to count the cost before we get out of the boat. God tells us that we should not go to war or try to build a tower without first counting the cost. If we start to build and are unable to finish, people will laugh at us. I have never been too concerned about the "boat sitters" laughing at me as I attempt to walk on water. I have been concerned only about one thing – is this the will of God? If so, I am prepared to deal with the possible negative consequences of the decision.

Usually, I think of the worst thing that can happen if the decision goes into the toilet. Is it bankruptcy? Is it the finger pointing of all the "boat sitters" saying "I told you so?" Once I have come to peace with the negative possibilities, I throw myself into the vision of acquisition. By aggressively embracing the potential negative, Cathy and I (with a lot of help from the Lord and bankers) have acquired about a hundred properties worth millions of dollars.

As I was preparing to speak at a convention, I heard the still, small voice of the Lord say, "Tell them you are a millionaire." I argued with the Lord as I could only see misunderstanding, jealousy and other negatives coming with such a pronouncement.

Nevertheless, God seemed insistent that I make this questionable proclamation, as I could not get it out of my mind.

"I want to tell you something that I have never said before in public," I stated.

"I heard God speak to me this morning as I was finishing my preparation for this message. He told me to tell you that I am a millionaire."

It was very quiet and everybody's attention was glued to the pulpit waiting for what was next. I told the people that God was no respecter of persons and that He did not love me more than them. Many of them were secret millionaires, as their farms were worth a lot.

I told them that I was an accidental millionaire as it was not my passion or purpose to become a millionaire but simply to serve the Lord with every ounce of my being. Many of us were "paper millionaires" because of the value of our acquisitions.

"He told me to tell you that I am a millionaire."

I challenged the conference attendees to believe God for more than they had and to take risks. Many businesses have a risk management department where workers' compensation and other insurance issues are addressed. Everybody who buys insurance is trying to manage their risk.

How much better if we allow the Lord to manage our risk! God risked everything to create us and give to us His nature of free will. Then He risked everything again to send His only Son to balance the books, conquer death and make a way for whosoever will.

Our God is a risk taker. For a committed Christian, risk taking is a faith venture.

I have a really good friend who tried to take his business to the next level. He has done hundreds of millions of dollars of business in the past twenty years. Prior to the economic meltdown of 2008, he was trying to break into the billionaire club.

We were determined to go out on the limb to find the blessing of the Lord.

It's just as spiritual for an obedient child of God to become a billionaire as it is to pastor a church, be a missionary or run a Christian school. God has anointed every born again believer with a ministry. There is not enough room for everybody to crowd around the pulpit on Sunday morning.

We have an invisible pulpit that goes wherever we go. In a book called *Loving Monday*, the author challenges his readers to understand that Monday is just as important as Sunday. Use what you do as a ministry to share Christ. The only Jesus that many people will ever see is the Jesus in you and me.

Many years ago when my wife and I bought a marina on Flathead Lake, Montana, we were overflowing with vision in the midst of the risk taking. We were determined to go out on the limb to find the blessing of the Lord. We jumped in and started a travel agency, law firm and restaurant in a building sitting on wooden stilts above the lake.

We recruited a friend to come and be the chef. We were confident that he was the best Italian chef in the world. We even named the restaurant after him, calling it "Rosario's." Our chef brought a prep cook and chief waiter with him. All three of these guys were moving in their gifting/ministry.

Soon we were up to our eyeballs in bills, bills and more bills. The food was fantastic but the bills were overwhelming us. We began to refer to food wholesaler Sysco as "the great Satan." We were upside down and owed Sysco about $5,000.

The local trade was small in this seasonal resort community. We were swimming in bills. We needed to make changes and make them fast. I called Sysco and told them to put us on COD until the balance was paid in full.

Although we were not making any money in our Italian restaurant, we added a pizzeria and a steakhouse. Now, we had three restaurants with different menus and immense possibilities. The food was great and we had a super team. We only had one major problem – we were still not making any money.

It is more about guts than bucks.

This was when I decided that I should develop an exit strategy. The casino where our steakhouse was located wanted to terminate our lease. Our manager was a committed believer that despised gambling (not a good fit) so we closed down the steakhouse. About the same time God sent us a buyer for the pizzeria, so we staggered onward with the Italian restaurant until we ended up selling the entire marina.

I have been asked many times by aspiring entrepreneurs what they needed most to get into business. I always tell them that it is more about guts than bucks.

Statistically, most businesses (just like marriages) fail in the first couple years. Thomas Edison spoke for all entrepreneurs and inventors when he was asked how it felt to have failed so many times in his effort to invent a light bulb. Edison said, "You are mistaken. I have never failed. I merely found out one more thing that does not work. I am one step closer to my goal."

Most of the wealthy people in the world are risk takers. The same is true for those who build large churches and ministries. A risk taker is committed to succeed where others have failed.

"Take chances, make changes."

When we were in the middle of our restaurant venture, I went to the local bank to try to secure a line of credit. We wanted to avoid the cash flow ups and downs so common in business. I was shocked that they turned me down.

Rejection by the bank did not stop me from going forward. I just switched to the "plastic bank" to carry us through the rough times. I don't recommend using credit cards but I know that true entrepreneurs will do whatever it takes.

Risk takers know that they need to get in or get out of the way. Our money and our mouth need to be in the same place.

God says that the word did not profit them, as it was not mixed with faith (Heb 4:2). God challenges us to do what He says. The Bible says that where your treasure is, there will your heart be also.

As I was praying, I sensed the Lord say, "Take chances, make changes." It has been a guiding principle throughout my life. My dad was scarred by the great depression, so he chose security.

Even before I accepted Christ, I decided to be an optimistic risk taker. Risk takers risk money, relationships, and being misunderstood. They are more than gamblers throwing dice or playing blackjack. Risk takers live beyond their comfort level.

Abraham was the ultimate risk taker when he took Isaac to Mount Moriah. He was prepared to sacrifice him pursuant to the Word of God. Esther too had the heart of a risk taker when she said, "If I perish, I perish."

Oftentimes risk takers have to overcome their initial reluctance. They have to battle through their fear of man, fear of failure or fear of unseen consequences. The risk taker thinks and acts differently than others.

The risk taker says, "It's only money," while others might say, "You could lose everything." The risk taker says, "What have you got to lose?" while most say, "Better safe than sorry." Mr. Risk Taker says, "You can always start over," while Mr. Better Safe Than Sorry says, "I'm too old to start over."

Joseph Bayly, wrote a motivational poem for all risk takers:

"Give me courage Lord to take risks, not
the usual ones – respected – necessary
– relatively safe,
But those I could avoid, the go for broke
ones.
I need courage, not just because I may fall
on my face or worse,
But others seeing me a sorry spectacle if it
should happen will say
'He didn't know what he was doing', or
'he's foolhardy ...'
When it comes right down to it Lord, I
choose to be your failure before anyone
else's success.
Keep me from reneging on my choice."
...Joseph Bayley, "Men's Devotional Bible",
Zonderan Publishing, 1993

Risk taking is more than buying and selling. Ultimately risk taking is all about believing that God is Jehovah Jireh. He is the provider who covers us when our banker says no. He is the Peace Giver when our risk taking raises fears within and without.

Ultimately there will be no blessing and no success without a willingness to take risks. It is one of the nearest and dearest keys that I think of when it comes to finding and receiving the blessing of the Lord.

17

Don't be Stopped by Bad Decisions

Position for Blessing - Make Good Decisions

FOR A BRIEF PERIOD OF TIME I worked as a director of development and property manager for a mission organization. I reported directly to the founder and director of the ministry who was a classic micro-manager. He was a good man who had worked hard to establish a ministry that reached around the world strengthening pastors and Christian workers.

In my job as the property manager I thought we should merge the positions of custodian and maintenance, thereby saving the ministry some money. I went ahead and terminated the existing commercial custodian and hired a man who I had found to be an excellent maintenance man.

About two weeks after hiring my friend, I found that he was an illegal alien (or "undocumented immigrant" for the PC police). I immediately went to my friend and told him that I would have to let him go as the Social Security card that he had given me was bogus. He offered to give me another card but I declined. I needed to eat some humble pie and go back to the original custodial service. Once the problem was all solved, I needed to report to my boss what had happened.

"I have a whole lot more bad decisions inside me waiting to get out."

I told my boss that I had made a bad decision in hiring an illegal alien to do the maintenance and custodial work but that I had cleaned it all up. And then I told him that I had some more bad news.

He looked at me with a "what's next" look. I told him, "I have a whole lot more bad decisions inside me waiting to get out." I thought this might bring a chuckle but all I got was a glare.

We all have a lot of bad decisions inside us just waiting to get out. We have classes for everything: math, science, mechanical arts, journalism, English, foreign languages, physical education, history, bookkeeping, creative writing, keyboarding and on and on. But, we have no class on decision-making. There was no class to teach us the ins and outs or do's and don'ts of good decision-making.

Many people are rendered impotent by the possible negative consequences of a bad decision. To find the blessing of the Lord, we need to become proficient at decision-making. How do we come from a place of double-mindedness or indecisiveness to be like Joshua?

Joshua spoke clearly and decisively when he said "as for me and my house we shall serve the Lord." We sometimes face big decisions where we need to counsel with those wiser than ourselves. These big areas include marriage, moving, money and ministry.

Some people make decisions by applying reason and logic. This is oftentimes done by making a pro/con list. Others choose to pray for wisdom and understanding. Sometimes prayer is nothing more than a decision-making delay tactic.

The Lord told Joshua to quit praying and get off his face and deal with the sin in the camp. Real prayer is not passive postponement but listening for the mind of Christ. The still, small voice of God spoke to Elijah when he was in the cave and He still speaks to us today.

Real prayer is not passive postponement.

Counseling is another way to make a decision. Counsel is much more than polling a circle of friends or advisors looking for somebody to say what you want. We need honest truth tellers courageous enough to tell us what we need to hear.

When I discerned the Lord's clear whisper, "Don't fire Bob, fire yourself," I needed to make a decision accordingly.

It reminds me of the guy who fell off the cliff and grabbed a tree limb on the way down. As he was hanging precariously to the tree, he hollered out, "God, help me."

He heard a voice that sounded like the voice of God say, "Just let go." Unsatisfied with the answer, the man hollered again, "Is there anybody else up there?"

Too many of us are just like the desperate man hanging to a tree limb calling out to God. When He answers, we don't like what He has to say so we look for a different voice.

Another method utilized to make decisions is to poll our family and friends. How many are for? How many are against? Many politicians attempt to make decisions by utilizing Gallup and other pollsters.

I heard an international evangelist say, "All decisions are emotional." Believing myself to be more cerebral, I initially rejected this statement. But the more I processed it, I could see that even those of us who thought we were creatures of logic, justified (and hid) our feeling decision behind intellectual statements of justification.

"All decisions are emotional."

In the Bible they cast lots for the replacement apostle. My wife often put an end to quarrelling among our children by flipping a coin to determine who received the last piece of cake. The National Football League uses coin flips to determine who receives the football first. Burgers or pizza? Flip a coin!

Some choose to make a decision on the basis of their experience. Experience is only a good teacher if we are listening to its voice. Insanity is defined as doing the same thing again and again while expecting a different result.

Micro-managers hold every decision. They favor centralization versus de-centralization. On the other hand, good decision making is often delegated to others who have a better grasp of the facts. Delegation is a great way to make a decision but it does not relieve the delegator of responsibility.

Some make decisions by rationalizing, "What will be, will be." This philosophy of fatalism is popular with those who want to escape personal responsibility. On the other hand, there are things that are strictly in the hand of God (such as the weather).

Others minimize by saying, "It's no big deal." Still others join the proverbial ostrich by putting their heads in the sand in an attempt to "ignore it." Rationalizing, minimizing and ignoring are tools for those who want to do little or nothing.

One of the most popular "Christian methods of decision-making" is called FLEECING. The practitioner of fleecing is following in the footsteps of Gideon and refuses to make a decision until God does something. Generally, fleecing is a method to be employed when all other methods fail. When Gideon "fleeced" God, it was to assuage his doubts and fears. When we have a clear word from God, we have faith and don't need to fleece.

Poor decisions are oftentimes the result of flawed or incomplete information. God is the source of all wisdom. Prayer for wisdom is just as important as gathering facts. Without His wisdom we will misinterpret the facts.

The Bible says, "Without counsel, plans go awry" (Prov 15:22). Seek counsel from the successful, the spiritual and those who know you. Too many who are hurting in their marriage go to the recently divorced rather than people who have been successfully married for 20 or more years. They are not looking for counsel to make a righteous decision but justification to do what they have already decided to do.

Seek counsel from the successful.

The Bible tells us to examine our hearts (1 Cor 11:28) for wrong motivations which lead to wrong decisions. "As a man purposes (or thinks) in his heart, so is he," asserts the Scripture.

As risk takers, my wife and I have prepared ourselves for the "worst case scenario." Proverbs says that "the preparation of the heart belongs to man but the answer of the tongue is of the Lord" (Prov 16:1). We need to humble ourselves as His servants who want His will more than our own. We do this by wiping away our primary desires so that we "delight ourselves in the Lord."

I envision my mind like a whiteboard (or blackboard if you want) that is wiped clean, waiting for the hand of God to write on my wall. When we empty ourselves of personal preferences, we have positioned ourselves for the mind of Christ (aka the will of God). Through humility we confess that we will do whatever He wants (Jas 4:10-15).

Good decision-makers have learned to stand still...

Once we have applied all relevant scripture, we make a decision for better or for worse. We walk by faith and not by sight. The peace of God governs and guides our lives.

Don't be in a hurry to make a decision. It's a process that is sometimes like having a baby. The facts, desires, Scripture, counsel and everything is mixed together where it grows daily. Those who are in a hurry usually make bad decisions. They mistakenly think any decision is better than no decision.

Good decision-makers have learned to stand still and see the salvation of the Lord. They have learned that fear is the opposite of faith. When I feel the torment of fear overtaking my head or my heart, I step back and pray. Any decision made in fear is sin.

We cannot blame others for bad decisions. Maturity requires that we accept responsibility for our bad decisions. God spoke to me, "As he is, so are we in this present world" (1 Jn 4:17). We must be willing to pay the price. Part of the price for a good decision is the process of waiting. It is during this time that we die to self and every selfish decision.

Good decision-making can be learned. It is imperative if you want to find His blessing that you align yourself completely and irrevocably with His Word. We know that His Word is His will.

Several years ago, President Bush was being questioned by a group of reporters about decisions that he had made in the war against terror. He said, "I am the decider in chief." Several reporters and commentators were offended by this remark but the President was right. He was elected to be the decider when it came to certain issues.

Many trial and error Christians could prevent bad things from happening by pre-thinking.

You also are called to be a decider of many issues. Your eternal destiny is decided by what you do with Jesus, the Christ. Your earthly destiny is decided by many lesser decisions, from obeying your parents and teachers, to postponing certain pleasures (owning a car, having sex, etc.), to assuming certain obligations (taking a job rather than pursuing an education).

Too many of us practice "trial and error" decision making. We don't pre-think what we will do if certain things happen. We become the tumbleweed blowing in the wind. Pragmatism is a humanistic philosophy that says if it works, it is good.

Many trial and error Christians could prevent bad things from happening by pre-thinking. God says that we are to prepare our hearts. We do this by pre-thinking solutions to certain situations. When the devil knocks on the door, we are prepared to have Jesus answer the door.

When a coach or player says, "It was my fault. I made poor decisions," God is pleased when we accept responsibility rather than trying to blame somebody. He wants His children to MAN UP and take responsibility for their actions.

Brother Lawrence in his small book, *"The Practice of The Presence of God,"* said that if anything good happened he thanked God and if anything bad happened he took the blame. This is what it means to man up.

If we are going to experience the consistent blessings of the Lord, we must learn to make good decisions. Every decision brings either a blessing or a curse. Every decision moves us forward or sets us back. Positioning for blessing demands that you become a good decision maker.

All of your decisions have gotten you where you are today. Do you like where you are? Good decisions are a key to blessing.

18

Don't Wait for the Spanking

Position for Blessing - Judge Yourself

SCRIPTURE SAYS THAT GOD SPANKS His own children as evidence of their legitimacy (Heb 12:5-17). God's sole motivation for spanking us is to help us grow up. It is one of God's methods for training us.

God changes us into His image and likeness through spankings. He spanked Adam and Eve when He sent them from the Garden of Eden. He spanked Moses and Aaron when by refusing to let them go into the Promised Land. He spanked David for committing murder and adultery.

Baby Christians are all about themselves. They believe that life revolves around them and their needs. They must be handled with care. Pouting and self-pity are common reactions when their will is crossed.

God crosses our will just like a parent, simply by saying, "No." No, you cannot buy that car. No, you cannot go to that party. Many immature adults have mastered the adult temper tantrum.

Baby Christians have messy diapers and refuse to feed themselves. Babies don't bathe themselves by the washing of the water of the Word. They need constant supervision and can't wait for anything. Every parent has looked at his child and said, "If you act like a child, I will treat you like a child."

God tells us to "put to death worldly members" (Col 3:5-17). We need to put to death fornication, uncleanness, passion, evil desires and covetousness. To "reckon" something as dead is to count it as dead. If it's dead, it no longer has a voice or a power to control or influence us.

Baby Christians are all about themselves.

We need to put off the old man of anger, wrath, malice, blasphemy, filthy language and lying to one another.

God expects to put on the new man of tender mercies, kindness, humility, meekness, long suffering, bearing with one another, and forgiving one another. God said that above all we need to put on love.

I am embarrassed when I think of how immature I was when I came to Christ in 1970. I had a short wonderful honeymoon with the Lord where God seemed so real and close that my life was one big smile.

My first major setback in my relationship with the Lord came with the posting of the first semester law school grades. I had never studied harder and was convinced that

God was going to put me at the top of the class. “I didn’t need you to get those grades. I could do that without any help from you,” I shouted at God.

My grades were so bad (C-) that I was angry and confused. This was the beginning of my six months of walking around the wilderness looking for an argument with whoever wanted to defend God.

For the first year of my walk with the Lord, I was a barstool Christian eating peanuts and drinking beer while sharing the goodness of God with whoever would listen. I was doing just that with a friend when he told me to shut up.

“There’s no difference between you and me. You drink Budweiser and I drink Budweiser,” argued my friend.

All my arguments of the inner man fell on deaf ears. My unbelieving friend challenged me to “put up or shut up.” I left the bar with a decision that my friend’s soul was worth a lot more than a bottle of Budweiser beer.

During the time of wandering in the wilderness, I heard Pastor David du Plessis, known as Mr. Pentecost, share, “God’s got a nursery for all the baby believers.” Prior to hearing that statement, I was content to walk in biblical ignorance. I believed the word in James that, “To him that knows to do good and doeth it not, it is sin.”

A boundary is a fence that you erect to show ownership of your life.

I thought I could be like the little monkey who saw no evil, heard no evil and spoke no evil. Ignorance was bliss until I was confronted with the possibility that I could spend eternity in Heaven's nursery. It was time to grow up.

Several years ago I was visiting some good friends in Sheffield, England. I noticed the stone hedges throughout the countryside. My friends told me that the stones were boundaries similar to barbed wires or fancy fences. The purpose of marking a boundary is to show ownership and stop trespassers.

Christians need to set biblical boundaries for how they are going to live. A boundary can be as simple as, "I don't read pornography," or, "I don't tell dirty jokes," or, "I don't flirt with anybody but my spouse." A boundary is a fence that you erect to show ownership of your life. It defines you as people look and say, "That's Joe, he is a believer that doesn't do pornography, tell dirty jokes or flirt."

Christianity is about freedom. Some are opposed to any and all rules believing that the rules take away their freedom. Although certain rules are joy stealers, rules are intended to protect you from danger. "Don't touch the burner" is a rule meant to keep children from burning their hand.

After looking at the hedges, my English friends took me to their small, historic Anglican church where I found a brochure about "Rogationtide Sunday." As a quasi-wordsmith, I love words and was immediately curious to know what the word "rogation" meant.

"Every year in the springtime, all the governmental leaders of the village would come to the church for the beginning of Rogationtide," explained my friend.

"But, what does it mean? I have never heard the word 'rogation' or 'Rogationtide,'" I asked.

"It was a time when the officials, along with the local vicar, walked the boundaries of the village. They would cover a different part of the boundary line each day until the entire village was circled," said my friend.

"So, they circled the village, but for what purpose?"

"They had two purposes. One was practical and one was spiritual. They wanted to make sure that all the boundary markers were still in place. The spiritual purpose was to stop and pray for God's blessing and protection on the village," explained my friend.

If you want to position yourself for God's blessing, you must judge yourself...

"Do they still do this?" I asked.

"No. It's part of the history but not part of the present practice."

"I can see such a wonderful application for individuals to have a personal boundary check where they make an annual examination and pray for blessing and protection," I concluded.

During my first year as a Christian, I had not set certain boundaries concerning drinking alcohol. I ended up drinking beer until my friend told me that there was no difference between him and me.

The Bible challenges us to judge ourselves. If we judge ourselves, we won't be judged. We are also supposed to "punish our disobedience." An appropriate interpretation is "don't wait for the spanking." Set some boundaries that are in alignment with the Word of God.

If you want to position yourself for God's blessing, you must judge yourself and punish your disobedience. Maybe it's time to bend over and give yourself a hard swat on your derrière.

19

The "Osha Mosha" Man

Position for Blessing - Be Filled with the Spirit

"DO YOU SPEAK IN TONGUES?" asked Brother Charles, a missionary to Mexico.

"I asked the Lord to baptize me in the Holy Spirit shortly after I came to Christ but all I got were two words – Osha Mosha." I explained.

"Hey, that's good. When I got baptized in the Spirit, I only got one word. You have twice as many words as me," said Brother Charles.

"But I am not even sure that God put those words in my mouth. I grew up Catholic and thought it might have been pig Latin or actually two words from my high school Latin class. I thought that I might have just made them up."

"Here's what you need to do – just keep saying your two words until God gives you more. He looks on your heart and He will be pleased by your desire to worship Him. If the words are made up, God will replace them with His own vocabulary."

"Okay. I can do that."

I soon became known as "the Osha Mosha man."

This was a real conversation that signaled the end of my wilderness walk. I had been hanging out in the wilderness for almost six months since getting mad at God over my mediocre law school grades. God used a missionary from Mexico to challenge me to use my limited prayer language.

I soon became known as "the Osha Mosha man." I was quick to lay hands and pray for anybody needing prayer. I found myself saying over and over again – osha mosha, osha mosha, osha mosha, osha mosha.

"What are you doing?" asked my brother.

"I am just doing what Brother Charles told me to do. I am praying in tongues. I don't know what "osha mosha" means but I believe God will do what He needs to do both in me and in those that I am praying for," I said.

Little kids were beginning to pray the "osha mosha" prayer. I could tell that the entire church was beginning to ask the Lord to give me a larger vocabulary. I just left it in the hands of the Lord and prayed with faith my simple "osha mosha" prayer.

A few months later I was back at law school and still praying the "osha mosha" prayer. One night, there were four of us sitting in a small circle praying and praising the Lord. Suddenly I felt a need to raise my arms to the Lord like a radio antennae. As soon as my arms were extended towards Heaven, I received an immediate sensation flowing through both arms.

A key to finding God's blessing is receiving whatever God wants to give you.

My personal Pentecost was far less dramatic than the 120 in the upper room but no less effective. I was a bit self-conscious about what transpired, and attempted to pretend nothing happened. However, my brother, future wife and brother-in-law were all aware that something dramatic had just happened.

God had dropped the whole load on me. I had more than two words in my spiritual prayer language. "Osha mosha" was lost in the vast vocabulary that God had put in my mouth. Now, I could pray in the Spirit trusting God to interpret and answer as He saw fit. I had gone from seeker to receiver in just a matter of seconds. All I had done was believe and receive.

A key to finding God's blessing is receiving whatever God wants to give you. The Holy Spirit was the greatest gift that could be given to us. Jesus promised to send the Comforter who would guide us into all truth. The Holy Spirit convicts the world of sin while He teaches and comforts us.

Jesus was led by the Spirit as He went into the wilderness. We need the leading of the Holy Spirit every day in order to make right decisions and go in the right direction. Paul said that our spirit bears witness to His Spirit.

There is only one unforgiveable sin in the Bible – blaspheming the Holy Spirit. Our fundamentalist brothers who have rejected present day Holy Spirit manifestations are not guilty of committing this sin. The only unforgiveable sin is to reject the convicting power of the Holy Spirit when He comes with salvation.

Being led by the Holy Spirit is one of the most exciting things in my life. He has led me to make hard decisions (e.g. "Don't fire Bob, fire yourself") and to travel to strange places (e.g. smuggling Bibles into China).

"Get your degree."

The Spirit has led me to give away money, buy buildings and speak prophetically over thousands of people.

Recently I was in Mexico at a camp when a young man came up to me and asked if I would pray over him. When people ask me to pray, it is a euphemism for prophecy. They want to know what God has to say to them. As I laid my hands on him, I had three words come to my mind, "Get your degree."

Normally my prophecies are more than three words. They are usually prophetic paragraphs pointing people into a certain direction. However, my constant prayer has been for brevity and accuracy.

"Lord, let the words be absolutely right on or totally wrong. Don't allow me to reach for the fortune cookie generalization of a little this and that," I have prayed.

I repeated the three words "get your degree" two more times so that I would feel better about the lack of length and breadth before opening my eyes (yes, I usually shut my eyes so that I will not be tempted to prophesy based on observation or body language). When I opened my eyes, the young man was crying as were all those around him.

"Why is everybody crying?" I asked one of the young men standing closest to me.

"This is my brother and he is in his final semester to become a medical doctor. He had become so discouraged that he had decided to quit medical school. He just came to this camp because I had urged him to come and seek the Lord. Now God has spoken specifically to him about what he is supposed to do," explained my friend.

Although I have prophesied thousands of times all over the world, I was staggered by God's faithfulness. I think that my faith was built more than that of the young man who was told to get his degree. I saw the young man a couple months later and he was happily studying hard and doing the grueling internship necessary to become a full-fledged doctor.

I am so humbled that God uses such an unsanctified vessel to speak His rhema word. I am nothing better than Balaam's donkey and yet He has chosen to use my obedient vocal chords.

I am nothing better than Balaam's donkey...

The first presbytery team that I ever participated in was in May, 1981 in Calgary, Alberta, Canada. God was faithful to allow me to have a clear word for a middle-aged couple.

"I see that you have had a bit of an argument over the presbytery. The woman of God wanted a new dress and you told her that she already has more than enough. I see a blue dress that she really wants but 'Mr. Cheapskate' has said you don't need it. God says, 'Buy her the blue dress,'" I prophesied.

The room exploded in joyful laughter, as unknown to me, the man was a banker and well known for his penurious tendencies. It was such a small thing but it showed the couple that God was concerned about the details of their lives. The banker went out and bought his wife the blue dress. I saw them about fifteen years later and the banker said, "Do you remember me?"

I confessed that I did not so he quickly reminded me of the prophetic meeting when I prophesied over him and his wife concerning the blue dress. "That was a turning point for me. I knew that God had so much more for me than just working as a banker. Now, I am an associate pastor and could not be happier," he explained.

The Holy Spirit uses all the gifts of the Spirit to change people into His likeness and image. I used to wrestle with trying to define whether something was a prophecy or word of knowledge. After allowing myself to be distracted by the academic nuances between prophecy and word of knowledge, I heard the Lord tell me, "Don't worry about labeling the gift."

The Lord went on to instruct me that the most important thing is to know that the word or gift comes from the heart of the Lord. Even as there is a blending and blurring of the fivefold ministry gifts in Ephesians 4:11-13, so is there a blending and blurring of the spiritual gifts set out in 1 Corinthians 12.

At the first prophetic presbytery, I made a significant error. After prophesying over a single man, I said, "If this does not happen in the next six months, call me!"

I forgot the instruction of my friend and prophetic mentor, Lin Perry, who said, "We shoot them (prophetically) and you (local leadership) clean them."

About a year later I was awakened in the middle of the night from a sound sleep by the sound of my phone ringing.

"Hello, this is Doug Kelley," I said

"Hey this is Joe from Calgary," the voice (presumably Joe) spoke.

"Hi Joe. How may I help you?"

"Do you remember me? You prophesied over me at the Full Gospel Church in Calgary," stated Joe.

"I can't picture you Joe. It's been about a year or so since I was with you in Calgary. How can I help you?" I asked.

"Well, you told me that if the prophecy did not come to pass within six months that I should call you. So I am calling you," Joe explained.

"I vaguely remember telling you to call me but I honestly do not even remember the substance of the prophetic word over you. I should not have told you to call me as your pastor and elders are the ones who need to judge, interpret and apply what was said over you," I explained apologetically before praying for him and hanging up.

God puts the words into the mouths of the prophets...

Live and learn by your mistakes and you are a wise man. I believe passionately in the Spirit and in the prophetic as one of the best modes of finding His will for our lives. We will never experience true and lasting blessing unless the Holy Spirit is given consistent opportunity to speak into our lives.

Prophecy is a gift of the Spirit that comes into the mouth and is delivered to the beneficiary. It is not something that comes to the mind but to the mouth.

There are times when a phrase is in my mind but it is not prophecy until the Lord opens my mouth and spills the word into the ear of the person it is intended for. It is not a clever compilation of carefully constructed words but a spilling forth. God puts the words into the mouths of the prophets before they deliver the revelation to the recipient.

He who speaks in an unknown tongue edifies himself. You build spiritual muscle when you speak in tongues the same way a weight lifter builds muscles by lifting weights. "Be strong in the grace of the Lord" is an admonishment to build spiritual muscle. We cannot do exploits for the Lord with mere physical muscle. We need the muscle that comes from exercising our faith.

Walking in the Spirit is so much fun. You never know when you might fall over with a genuine belly laugh. My brother Don and I were teamed up to pray and prophesy over folks at the end of a meeting. Lines formed in front of each of the different teams. A short couple came forward for us to minister to them.

I was grasping with the correct prophetic word to describe what I was seeing in the Spirit.

"I am trying to find the right word to describe what I am seeing. It's like a 'grain bin,'" I said as I wrestled for the exact word to describe the prophetic vision.

"I know! Leprechauns!" blurted out my brother in an effort to help bring clarity to the prophetic vision. He thought I said "green men" and based on their short stature, leprechauns seemed reasonable.

"No, you idiot! It's an elevator," I stated as our line melted away. We quickly attempted to clean up the mess we made by praying for the couple. Afterwards, I noticed that our line was gone as everybody moved to another line where there appeared to be more prophetic anointing.

"Hey, we have room in our line," I announced to those in the other line as they looked away and pretended not to hear. I looked at my brother and said, "The heck with them. Let's go eat a cookie and have a cup of coffee."

We went to the showers early just like a pitcher that was having a hard time finding the strike zone. We have laughed repeatedly over the "little green men" prophecy. The Bible says that a merry heart is medicine. We might have missed the strike zone with our prophecy but we found humor to last a lifetime.

We have laughed repeatedly over the "little green men" prophecy.

Another time Cathy and I had one of those devil-inspired arguments just before we went to church. As we waited for the Spirit to speak, I sensed God wanted me to bring forth a gift in tongues requiring an interpretation. I had never done this before (or since) and was very nervous as I began to speak with some Chinese-sounding tongue.

Cathy was positive that I had overstepped my grace and would be rebuked for speaking out of turn. However, God had another plan. The pastor brought a strong interpretation that was especially applicable to Cathy. God uses His gifts as power tools to grow us into His image and likeness. They are not toys but tools meant to build the body of Christ.

I have found a real joy in prophesying over unbelievers. I usually tell them that I want to pray for them and then begin to minister whatever God has given to me. I know that many people are more comfortable asking than simply praying. I have found that it is less awkward if I just close my eyes, extend my hand and begin praying for them.

When you see God move, run over and put your hands out.

It is not unusual for the unbelieving recipient of a prophetic prayer to be blessed to tears. We used to invite political candidates to come to our church prior to the election to be introduced to our congregation. The highlight was when we called them forward to receive a gift (usually a Bible) and a blessing. The presence of the Lord was so strong that even the unbelievers could sense something special.

"How can I be more used by the Spirit of God?" I asked Brother Earl Kellum – an old apostle from Mexico who was known for his ability to hear the Spirit of God and prophesy non-stop for hours.

"There is no big secret. When you see God move, run over and put your hands out. It's not about you. It's all about Him. It's His Spirit that does the work. All we do is agree with His Spirit," explained Brother© Kellum.

I have never forgotten that advice. I am always looking for a true move of the Holy Spirit so that I can run over and put my hands out. I want to be a co-laborer with the Lord. I want to see His Spirit change lives, especially my own.

Many of the keys to being blessed have to do with you making a decision or doing something. This chapter challenges you to listen to the voice of God's Spirit as He speaks through the gifts of the Spirit. He wants to give you His counsel. You get to accept it or reject it.

Positioning for blessing requires you to pray for ears to hear the voice of God.

20

The Most Negative Person

Position for Blessing - Reach Others

"YOU ARE THE MOST NEGATIVE PERSON that I have ever known," said my wife to our church administrator.

"I don't have to stand here and take that. I can sit down and take it," joked Kert.

"Kert, we so appreciate everything you have done for us, for the church and for the House of Hope. However, you can't just keep putting down the people. They are changing," explained Cathy.

"Hey, I think all they are doing is conning you and Doug. They see him as nothing but Santa Claus. They want the rich white guy to give them something. Every person, except Larry and Kesha, has his hand out," explained the most negative man ever known.

"They are changing. We see it, even if the changes are small," said Cathy.

"Tell me one person who has really changed. I can't think of one person," argued Kert.

"Well what about you? You've changed."

If beauty is in the eye of the beholder, Kert sees little beauty in the ministry to the lost, the least and the lonely of South Central Los Angeles. Is he right or is he wrong? Should we shake the dust off our beat-up shoes and weary feet and move on to greener pastures?

Even as the Lord spoke to me in 1984 that the church had become monastic and needed to go back to the marketplace, Open Arms is firmly entrenched in the marketplace. It is not settled in the suburbs or among the clean, rich comfortable people, but the poor, homeless and addicted.

Open Arms is firmly entrenched in the marketplace.

God does not override our free will but, in a real sense, the ministry chooses us as much as we choose it. In my own sense of logic, I would not go to the type of people that make up the Open Arms church family. I would go to up and outers rather than down and outers.

Working with the poor and addicted is a daily challenge. I have long taught that poverty and shame come to those who refuse instruction. Jesus said that we would have the poor with us always. Many years ago, I began an adult

Sunday School lesson with a quote from a well-known Christian author and businessman.

"If you live in America and you are not rich, you are either incredibly lazy or incredibly stupid," said the wealthy Christian businessman.

"That is the most offensive statement that I have ever heard. He is arrogant and he is wrong. I can't believe that you have even used it," an older member of the Sunday School angrily stated.

"I agree that he is arrogant, but is he wrong?" I asked.

We went on to have a very dynamic conversation about work, money and poverty. There is no question that the rich, arrogant Christian friend was wrong theologically. The curse of poverty claims individuals, families and nations.

God's will for your life involves people.

God says if you walk with a fool, you become a fool. If you walk with wise men, you will become wise. God has called Christians to reach beyond their comfort level and to go outside the camp.

God's will for your life involves people. Man was created to have relationship with both His creator and the other created beings. We were not created to be an island. Every man is like a finger connected to a hand. As a finger you are unique, but you are also connected to the rest of the hand which makes you part of a group.

The Greek or Western mindset focuses on the individual while the Hebrew or Eastern mindset focuses on the group. Both perspectives are valid. If we go overboard on either side, we will miss the most important mindset – the mind of Christ.

In 1984, most churches were focused on building bigger and better bless-me clubs emphasizing internal ministries like worship, teaching and children.

My book about going *From the Monastery to the Marketplace* received several rejections before I threw it in a bottom drawer and moved on. (It's about to be rewritten, resurrected and published on the heels of this book.) Today there are many well written, challenging books pushing the church to go outside its four walls and much of the church has responded.

For many Christians it is scary to interact with people who talk, think and act different than them. Many have told me how much they want to work for a "Christian company" as if it would make their lives easier.

I have found that most Christians do not want to be held to a higher standard when they are working for a Christian company. They expect to be "given grace" to show up late, leave early, receive and make personal calls, and be paid more than the heathen.

Many years ago I owned a building with my law partner and two realtors. The building needed some work done, so I suggested we hire Les who was a deacon/handyman from my church. After Les accepted the job and was working, I had a conversation with one of my partners.

"I am not happy with the work that your man is doing on the repair," stated my partner.

"Have you told him that you are not satisfied with his work?" I asked.

"Yeah, I talked to him about a week ago but it did not seem to make any difference."

"Well, then let's get rid of him. Do you want me to fire him?" I asked.

"No. You can't do that. He is a deacon in your church and your friend."

"That does not justify him doing a bad job. If anything, he should do a better job because he's a Christian and a friend. I will speak to him now. If the problems are not solved in the next couple of days, I will fire him."

A boss has a great opportunity to teach people to be productive citizens.

I immediately went to the handyman/deacon and told him that he needed to correct the problems ASAP or I was going to have to "let him go." He appeared shocked and said that he would get right after it. A few days later, I asked my real estate partner if the changes were acceptable. He just shook his head.

"Hey, Les, my partner is still not satisfied so you need to pack it up. We will pay you for what you have done. We are going to hire somebody else to finish up," I said.

"But I thought I was doing what he wanted. I made the changes he was concerned about," explained Les.

"Well, it's still not acceptable so we need to move in another direction. Give me your bill for services and I will cut you a check," I said.

"So, you are actually firing me?" he asked.

"I would rather say, 'It's not working out and we need to go our separate ways," I explained.

As I paid Les for the work that he had done, I told him that I had another job for him if he was interested. Les accepted the job working on my house but did not do much better. The God of the second chance never quits investing in His children.

Hiring people is exciting as you are moving in faith for the person and the task that they have been hired to do. Firing can be a downer, as there is no joy in the Promised Land, only the reality that it's time to part ways.

I believe that a boss has a great opportunity to teach people to be productive citizens. They can do more by firing somebody than grumbling and carrying them along when they are not doing their job.

My church administrator Kert has hired and fired many folks in the past couple of years as we have been building and remodeling some of the property that we own. He is known for his cynicism.

"I am tired of hiring ghetto people who do ghetto work. They say that they can do something that they have never done and then they do it all wrong," complained Kert.

"Well, we are training them. You are super-talented and can teach them how to do the job," I explained.

"I don't want to teach them. It's easier for me to just go do it right the first time than allow them to flounder around making a mess of everything."

"You used to train people at UCLA how to do their job. You can teach our folks how to build or repair something."

"What part of NO do you not understand? I don't want to teach them. They need a pastor but I'm not him. I will help you, but I am not interested in being sucked into the ghetto quagmire of over-promising and under-delivering," concluded Kert.

For over ten years Kert has been the most loyal and giving friend. He has been the church photographer, sound man, bookkeeper, electrician, plumber, repairman, administrator, video man and everything else needed at Open Arms, House of Hope, or Kelley properties. He tells people that he does "whatever Doug does not do or want to do."

The church needs to get its hands dirty...

During this time Kert has remained loyal to me and critical of "the flock." He models love, service, loyalty, honesty and dependability. Nevertheless, he has also distinguished himself as super-critical and negative.

The church needs to get its hands dirty by mixing it up with the needs of a society and culture that are suspicious of the religious right and the "born agains." God uses whoever and whatever is available. Kert is both the object of God's affection and a tool in the hands of God.

Kert was baptized a Methodist and sang "Kum Ba Ya" at the youth group. However, his faith level and practice could be more described as superficial. He went to UCLA, got married and had two children. His work ethic and abilities caused him to oversee 2000 people and a hundred million dollar budget while employed at UCLA. However, when his marriage fell apart, he found no solace in the church but in the bottle.

Like so many who are caught in a downward spiral, Kert's life went from divorce to drinking to destruction. He pled guilty to a charge of domestic abuse against the neighbor that he began living with after his divorce. As he sat in a Los Angeles jail cell, he was given an opportunity to join a recovery program. Kert jumped on the get-out-of-jail-free card even though the program was faith-based.

God's blessing is entwined with repaying our debt to the Greek and the barbarian.

Kert has probably heard more messages about Jesus than anybody else at Open Arms during the past six years. He has had people prophesy over him, praise him and befriend him. Nevertheless, he is reluctant to fully embrace the basic tenets of the Christian faith. He has looked at the hypocrisy of those who say they believe but their lives continue to be full of drugs and deception.

"Before I kick the bucket, I want to water baptize you," I told Kert.

"I was baptized as a baby," he responded.

"That doesn't count. You had nothing to do with it. A Christian baptism is an expression of faith in the Lord made by those who have received Him," I explained.

"Don't hold your breath," Kert concluded.

Why include a negative name-calling ex-bureaucrat like Kert in a book that extols the principles of positioning yourself for blessing? It's because God's blessing is entwined with repaying our debt to the Greek and the barbarian. He has called us to worship and serve Him by showing His nature to those who live outside of the sanctuary of the Lord.

Kert is an astute observer of Christian behavior. He has observed the inconsistencies that we sometimes call "hiccups." He has looked at what our people call Christianity and said, "If that is Christianity, I don't want it."

I have called Kert "my focus group of one." He brings a different perspective to what we Christians do. His mind and past are not immersed in "Christian-ese" so he thinks and sees differently.

If it's our objective to reach those outside of the camp, we need to have somebody interpret what they think. Kert is like many outside of the church. They have an opinion about everything and everybody. He has written his own commandments.

One of Kert's commandments is: "Kert is not a bank, so don't ask." In another commandment Kert says, "Thou shalt not get mad if Kert says No. If Kert says Yes, consider it a miracle." Kert has many other commandments that are humorous, cynical or negative.

The life of blessing is about looking for opportunities to do good.

Like Kert, many of our family and friends are full of sarcasm and cynicism. They are primarily concerned about their own lives. They want those that they meet to stay in their own lanes. There is a measure of wisdom in the commandments but much of it is a stiff-arm to those who are hurting.

God has called us to win the lost. They come in all sizes and shapes but they all come with their baggage whether it is addiction, pride, stubbornness or something else.

Blessing does not come by being self-absorbed and self-focused. The life of blessing is about looking for opportunities to do good. God has sent us to be a drink offering to the lost, the least and the lonely.

God gave us a special song that says it all. We refer to the song as the *Open Arms Song.* Cathy and I joined with anointed worship leader/songwriter, John Syratt, and wrote this song at an Open Arms Worship Seminar over ten years ago. Look carefully at the words. Our prayer is that we might become His "open arms showing people the way."

Open Arms Song

If it wasn't for Your mercy Lord
Where would I be? *(3x)*
Oh Lord, where would I be
Thank you for Your mercy Lord
You have rescued me
Thank you for Your open arms
You've accepted me
Thank you for Your power Lord
You have set me free
Oh Lord, You have rescued me
Let me be Your open arms
Reaching out today
Let me be Your open arms
Showing them the way
Let me be Your open arms
This is what I pray
Oh Lord, help me show the way

By John Syratt, Doug and Cathy Kelley

21

I'M ALL IN

Position for Blessing - Commit Everything

IN A DREAM, I SAW MYSELF sitting at a poker table with several others. I was holding my hand close to the chest so that none of the other players might get a peek. As I looked at my cards, I knew that I had the winning hand. Nobody was going to beat me. It was my turn to clean up.

In the dream I was waiting for my turn. I saw one guy raising, another calling, and another folding. Now it was my turn. All eyes were on me to see what I would do. I looked at the growing pot, pushed all my chips into the center of the table and said, "I'm all in."

Before I could see what everybody else did in response to my going "all in," I woke up. The dream was so vivid that

I felt like I was there playing poker. However, I had not played poker for forty years and do not ever remember going "all in."

"Lord," I prayed, "Show me the meaning of this dream. Let me know what you are trying to tell me."

Immediately, God spoke the interpretation, "The winning hand is the church. You are holding on to the one thing that means the most to Me. You are holding on to the church. If you go all in to the church, you will win much more than a game of cards and few dollars. You win everything when you go all in to the church."

The Spirit of the Lord began to teach me what it means to be all in. All in is more than a decision made by poker players. Church attenders need to decide if they are going to go all in. Family members, workers and recovering addicts also need to decide if they are going to go all in.

The Bible shows that the first disciples were of "one heart and one soul" (Acts 4:32-35). They held all things in common and there was "no lack." They laid their gifts at the feet of the apostles. In a very real sense these disciples were "all in."

You win everything when you go all in to the church.

Into this eclectic environment came the pretenders Ananias and Sapphira. They shouted amen when others brought their money and laid it at the feet of the apostles. They were so motivated that they went and sold their own property. But then they made a tragic mistake – they decided to lie to the Holy Spirit.

"Here is all our money from the sale of our property. We are all in," boasted Ananias as he laid the money at the feet of the apostles.

"Oh, my brother Ananias, did you not know that the property belonged to you as did all the money that you received when you sold it? But you have decided to lie to the Holy Spirit as to what you sold the property for. You lie, you die," said the apostle receiving the gifts. As the young men came back from carrying the dead body of Ananias out, his wife Sapphira arrives.

"Hello, Sapphira. Your husband just brought money from the sale of your property. He said that you sold it for $5,000 (my guesstimate). Is that correct?"

It takes commitment to stretch out and buy the field.

"Yes, that is the right amount of money," said Sapphira.

"Do you not realize that both the property and the money was yours to do with as you saw fit? However, you have lied to the Holy Spirit. Here come the young men who carried your husband's body to the grave."

Ananias and Sapphira are like many Christians who like to be around the smells and bells. They like to pretend that they are all in when they are merely playing religious games.

Matthew 13:44 says that when the man found the treasure in the field, he went and sold all that he had so that he could buy the field. It takes commitment to stretch out and buy the field. Ananias and Sapphira did not buy the field. Jesus is the treasure in the field while the field represents the church.

Like a worldly field, God's field (the church) has rocks and weeds. We are given authority to be "rock pickers" in the church. Everything is not perfect in the church but it is "Heaven on earth." A pastor is really a professional rock-picker.

God has said, "Don't pull up the weeds." Let them grow right along with the wheat. If we try to pull the weeds, we will also pull up the wheat. God says, "Leave it alone. I will sort it all out at harvest time."

True disciples of the Lord Jesus Christ buy the field. They don't wait for a perfect field free of rocks and weeds. They simply say the field is the bride of Christ and I am going to be a part of the bride for better or for worse.

They were caught by the "someday syndrome."

In Luke 9:57-62 there are three disciples that I call Mr. Too Soft, Mr. Too Slow and Mr. Too Busy. Jesus invited each of these disciples to come follow Him. However, they all had different excuses why they could not drop everything and just follow the Lord.

They were caught by the "someday syndrome." Someday I will tithe. Someday I will serve the Lord. Someday I will follow Jesus. None of these servants were all in.

Timid and fearful people spend time counting the cost instead of paying the price. Earlier we noted that successful companies had a bias for action. Procrastination is the sin of those mesmerized by indecision. Too many of God's people live with regret. "If only" they had done this or that, they reason after the fact.

Successful people seize the day. The only Latin they know is "carpe diem." They are moved with a sense of immediacy and refuse to be sucked into the "paralysis of analysis."

In a real sense, you have to get off your "butts" if you are going to go ALL IN. The Bible says "our desire is killing us" (Prov 21:25-26). Many of us are "mañana people," believing that we can do it tomorrow. Tomorrow is the busiest day of people's lives. Don't delay what you can do today.

The Bible is full of procrastinators with excuses why they could not just do what the Lord asked. "Who am I?" asked Moses. "What shall I say?" What if they do not believe me?" Moses concluded his questions with a plea that God send somebody else.

Isaiah focused on himself rather than God's sufficiency. He said, "I am undone. I am a man of unclean lips." God touched Isaiah's lips and said, "Your iniquity is taken away; your sin is purged" (Is 6:7). Isaiah was out of excuses so he said, "Here am I, send me."

Jonah was the ultimate procrastinator. He heard God clearly and then ran in the opposite direction before yielding to the dealing of the Lord to go to Nineveh. Doubting Thomas procrastinated in simply believing God.

In his excellent book, *Purpose Driven Life,* Rick Warren tells us that life on earth is but a dot while eternity is like a line. As Jesus was about the Father's business, we too must be about the "Father's Business." Our life is all about choices. Sydney Harris said, "Regret for the things we did can be tempered by time; it is regret for the things we did not do that is inconsolable."

Being all in is a prophetic challenge to become something more than lukewarm. The good news is that many of God's children have said "I'm all in."

Here are a few of those who were all in: Abraham left his family because he was all in; Noah built an ark because he was all in; Esther risked her life because she was all in; Shadrach, Meshach and Abednego were all in and went in faith to the fiery furnace; Daniel went to the lion's den; Peter walked on water; and Jesus carried the cross and accepted the nails because He was all in.

In the beginning of this book, I shared the story of conflict with my former friend. It was a painful time because the love I had for my friend was real as was the separation. A year after God had spoken to me in the dream about being "all in," I was in the middle of the painful, legal lawsuit with my ex-friend.

Satan loves flat-nosed, undiscerning Christians who refuse to judge right from wrong.

Many friends stood around as stoic spectators saying little or nothing. Many of those who spoke would only say that they are "praying for the situation." Of course, it is always good to pray, but for many it was nothing more than a religious mechanism to avoid making a decision.

Many Christians are quick to quote Satan's favorite scripture, "Judge not lest you be judged" (Matt 7:1). This verse would be better interpreted if we used the word "condemn" in place of judge as there are three distinct aspects to judgment: judge, discern and condemn. Satan loves flat-nosed, undiscerning Christians who refuse to judge right from wrong.

I found that I was nauseated by the side-stepping, conflict-avoiding perspective of many who considered themselves friends of both me and my ex-friend.

What happened to the challenge of restoration "if a brother be overtaken in a fault" (Gal 6:1)? During this time, I asked the Lord to keep my heart right as He worked on those who were busy straddling the fence between who was right and who was wrong.

I heard the still, small voice of God say. "There is no Switzerland in the Bible." The Swiss made a deliberate decision during World War II to remain neutral. They wanted to be the world's bankers, receiving money from both Germany and the Allied Forces. The Swiss refused to even speak out against the atrocities of Hitler.

Jesus said that you are "either for me or against me." You are either gathering or scattering. You cannot serve God and money (Matt 6:24). A double-minded man is unstable in all his ways.

"There is no Switzerland in the Bible."

Pontius Pilate made an effort to proclaim his innocence at the same time that he was consenting to the crucifixion of Jesus, King of the Jews. Pilate washed his hands as an open show of his innocence but the water could not remove the blood stains of his feigned neutrality.

God is building an unstoppable church that refuses the cowardly temptation of feigning neutrality. God has called believers to pick up their crosses and follow Him. We are called to be commitment Christians who lay our lives down like the forefathers in the faith who are memorialized in

Hebrews 11. Patrick Henry cried, "Give me liberty or give me death."

In the house of God there are no bleachers for spectators to sit on their excuses for non-involvement. It's easy to tell those who are all in. They are those who have joined the Fellowship of the Unashamed. Listen to these words from an African pastor and make them yours:

> *"I'm part of the fellowship of the unashamed. The die has been cast. I've stepped over the line. The decision has been made. I'm a disciple of His and I won't look back, let up, slow down, back away or be still.*
>
> *My past is redeemed. My present makes sense. My future is secure. I'm finished with low living, sight walking, small planning, smooth knees, colorless dreams, tamed visions, mundane talking, cheap living and dwarfed goals.*
>
> *I no longer need pre-eminence, prosperity, position, promotion, plaudits or popularity. I don't have to be right, first, tops, praised, regarded or rewarded. I now live by faith, walk by patience, lift by prayer and labor in His power.*
>
> *I won't give up, shut up, let up, until I have stayed up, stored up, prayed up, paid up and preached up the cause of Christ. I must go till He comes, give till I drop, preach till all know and work until He stops me. And when He comes for His own, He'll have no problem recognizing me – for my banner will be clear!"*

For a long time, I envisioned reaching the city of Los Angeles by buying a hotel and assembling a team of committed Christian workers to serve the needs of the brokenhearted. Our intention would be to literally live as a drink offering among the most needy in our community. In furtherance of this vision, I dragged my wife and others through many rundown hotels and different buildings that I thought might be suitable for this grand mercy vision.

We found nothing. My wife suggested we move into the small apartment located above our storefront church in South Central Los Angeles. I scoffed at her suggestion, as it was not grand enough or safe enough. In April, 2009 as I was having a quiet time in my nice, safe home in Orange County, California, I heard the voice of God.

"It's time to move to the city. Pack your bags. Go be Emmanuel (God with us)," spoke the voice of the Lord.

I was stunned. How could I take my wife to such an unsafe place? I really did not have any fear but was concerned about my duty to provide for and protect my wife.

When I told Cathy that it was time to move to the city, she said, "What happened to change your mind?

"We have told God that we would do whatever and go wherever He sent us. I just heard Him say move to the city," I explained.

"It's time to move to the city. Pack your bags. Go be Emmanuel (God with us)."

We packed our bags and moved to a place that housed a combination of African Americans and Hispanics. It had zero percent Caucasians. We lived in our small apartment above the church for over three years.

During our time living in South Central, we heard gunfire almost daily, saw a man get shot and had a bullet pass through our window, lodging in the wall adjacent to our refrigerator. Many of our friends asked us if we were afraid. Our answer was always the same loud, faith-filled NO! God was our source, our defender and protector. He would not allow anything to come against us that we could not handle.

Many years ago I was known among my friends and co-laborers for pushing as hard as I could to accomplish as much as I could. My friend, John Syratt, called it "Doug-it-to-the-max."

I have slowed down considerably since those days when I thought we should begin every conference or camp meeting with a 6:00 a.m. prayer meeting followed by a litany of meetings intended to transfer anointing and information from the "haves" to the "have-nots." I believed that vacations and days off were for the lazy and uncommitted.

Now, I am sixty-eight, slowing down and wanting more vacation and days off. My zeal has been moderated by time, energy and obesity. I have found great success in most areas of my life but still struggle with being overweight. I am blessed to be strong and healthy even though I want to lose 30 pounds yesterday.

Cathy and I have looked at many of our friends who have earned their retirement from many years of faithful labor. However, we still want to keep on praying, preaching and giving to those that the Lord has called us to love and shepherd. The Open Arms House of Hope recovery ministry drains us with those who choose heroin over Jesus. We battle through our weariness and look at those that are being helped.

In February, 2011, I signed a settlement agreement with my ex-friend. He agreed to pay for damages done to me. The total amount was close to $400,000. So far, he has only paid $9000. What would the Lord have me to do?

The key to finding God's blessing is to go ALL IN. Somebody said, "If God does not have all of you, He has none of you." The key to positioning for blessing is to know above all else that God is the Commander in Chief. He is in charge of your life, your ambitions and your future.

Many of the folks in our Open Arms Church want to get saved again every time a call for salvation is extended. I tell them that it is a one-time transaction. If you truly repented of your sins and received Christ into your heart, you don't need to do it again. However, there is a need to recommit every day in every way. Is Jesus Lord over every decision? Over your finances? Over your time? Over your relationships?

By now, you know me better than people who grew up with me because you have read about my successes and failures. You have read about my ambitions, fears and dreams. You have chosen to stay with me on a journey to living successfully under the leadership and Lordship of Jesus Christ.

The key to finding God's blessing is to go ALL IN.

Although I have shared twenty-one different things for you to do to position yourself for blessing, there is no simple formula that will insure your success or bring you His blessing. In the 1970s, Governor Jerry Brown of

California (aka Governor Moonbeam) preached his personal gospel of "less is more."

God says it differently. For Him to increase, we must decrease. For us to find our lives, we must lose our lives. If we want to be true disciples of Jesus, we need to deny ourselves and pick up our crosses.

I have had the privilege of travelling the globe and seeing God's plan and provision for people all over the world. Very few enjoy the blessings that we in America take for granted. We throw away daily more than most of them have in a month. I don't feel guilty for being born in America but I accept it as a call to "do good to all men."

I don't want to sit on a beach eating bon-bons while the world goes to hell...

Only God knows how many years each of us will live. It is our time to make a difference. It is our time to "do good." All that I have belongs to Him. I don't want to sit on a beach eating bon-bons while the world goes to hell in a hand-basket. I want to be salt and light to a lost and dying generation.

Cathy and I are ALL IN until death do us part. Do we get it right every day? Of course not! But, when we find that we have been holding back, we repent and recommit.

Only God is my source. I look to Jesus from whence comes my help. He is the author and finisher of my faith. I AM ALL IN. What about you?

Also by Doug Kelley

Relevant Rantings – A Daily Devotional

From the Monastery to the Marketplace

Open Arms – House of Miracles

With Larry Harris

The Voice of Hope – A Recovery Devotional

31108479R00165

Made in the USA
San Bernardino, CA
02 March 2016